The Bread and Butter Book

By Diana Sutton

The Good Life Press LTD

Published by
The Good Life Press Ltd.
PO Box 536
Preston
PR2 9ZY

www.goodlifepress.co.uk
www.homefarmer.co.uk

Set by The Good Life Press Ltd.
Additional illustrations by Rebecca Peacock
Printed and bound in Great Britain
by Cromwell Press

The Bread and Butter Book

By Diana Sutton

Dedication

This book is dedicated to my mum, Millicent Sutton.
She taught me what great happiness and contentment
can be found in baking.

Contents

The Staff of Life

Throughout history bread, or derivations of bread, have comforted and sustained us. It is an essential weekly purchase and a 'must have' in all but a few households. Its versatility made it a snack food eaten 'on the hoof' long before the idea of fast food became a feature of the high street. We feed it to our children when they are beginning to feed themselves and it is often the main item in their lunch boxes when they go to school.

A slice of toasted bread is the only thing I could ever face early in the morning before going to work and it remains a favourite breakfast and supper food in our house. Whilst the smell of freshly baked bread has a strong, emotive pull, a lettuce sandwich eaten a few hours before retiring is also an old remedy for aiding sleep.

The great thing about bread is that one never tires of eating it as it comes in so many different forms, flavours and textures. It is a useful ingredient in many recipes from sandwiches to breadcrumbs and as a binding agent in sausages and puddings and is also used to coat many foods before frying. The versatility of bread is easily overlooked as it is often under used in other recipes.

It is my hope in writing this book that more people will be encouraged to go back to making their own bread in as natural a way as possible.

It is clear, after talking to many different kinds of people from school children and teachers to friends of all ages, that most of us love the idea of homemade bread and everyone is impressed that it can be done so easily.

The purpose of this book is not to explain how to use bread-making machines as their use is often self-explanatory and, though they are widely used, I hope that this book will inspire the reader to make bread using their own hands. Having said this, I do feel for those who find kneading dough difficult and a mixer using dough hooks can be very useful.

So do enjoy reading this and enter into a new era of bread eating and bread making.

Diana Sutton
Manchester 2008

The Bread and Butter Book

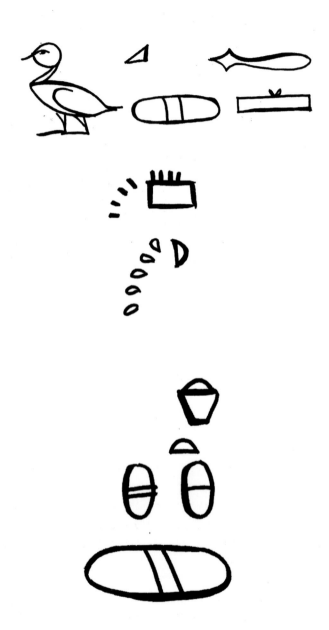

8

Bakers 'peel' or long shovel.

Chapter One
A Short (crust) History

Baking with grain based foodstuffs can be traced back to the Middle East in approximately 17,000 BC and archaeological work has found evidence of the organised arable farming of grain in 10,000 BC.

Ancient Egyptian artefacts prove that growing wheat for bread was widespread and there is artwork and hieroglyphic evidence of the use of grain in everyday food production.

Nearer to home, in Britain, we were making bread in the Stone Age using an ancient form of wheat called Emmer which was similar to Durum wheat that is used in the making of pasta.

Until the Roman invasion all dough was cooked on an open fire in Britain. What the Romans 'did for us' was to introduce enclosed ovens similar to the large pizza ovens we use today. Wheat was still the most popular grain used in bread making, however, when the Romans departed, the use of wheat declined and rye became more popular due to its higher yield.

In the Middle Ages bread was a status symbol, the rich eating 'Manchets' which were whiter, wheaten loaves whilst the poor ate a darker, coarser bread called 'Maslin which was made from rye but also often contained weed seeds, ground legumes and sometimes even acorns.

So important was bread as a source of food that through periods of harsh weather when crops of cereal failed, severe famines occurred causing widespread revolt. As a result, the ruling classes attempted to prevent the prices of grain and bread from rising too high.

In the nineteenth century the price of grain still had a great impact on society. The government stated that England was not allowed to import 'corn' [a word used to cover all grains] until its price rose above a certain level. This was to protect the English landowners who grew grain from losing out to cheaper foreign products.

The workers, unable to feed their families because of the cost of bread, protested and rose up, resulting in the powerful and influential anti-Corn Law movement. After much unrest the unpopular Corn Laws were removed and landowners had to compete with cheap foreign imports of grain, therefore having to grow their wheat more efficiently.

The significance of bread as a food staple carried on throughout the twentieth century when the allocation of bread to the troops in two world wars became a necessity and feeding people at home was more difficult. Governments have even used bread as a means of providing the people with a balanced diet by adding certain vitamin supplements to mass-produced loaves.

In fact no other single foodstuff has carried so much continuous historical importance as our beloved loaf.

These days bread is still a staple food in our diet and there is a great variety of flour and ready made bread available to us in the shops. It is a valuable source of carbohydrates, many necessary vitamins and minerals and, to a lesser degree, protein. Bread makes a quick meal in our very busy lives and people with a gluten free diet can still enjoy eating a loaf made with gluten-free flour. This is a blend of grains using rice, tapioca, potato and maize flours.

Although most people in the UK buy their bread from large supermarkets, small artisan bakers' shops as seen throughout France are making a comeback with big chain bakers remaining commercially successful by selling pies and many other traditional items baked 'in-store.'

I still get a thrill from seeing a local baker with a

shop full of their own baked bread and each one often having a signature loaf baked to a secret recipe known only to their family.

We also have the added luxury of enjoying bread products from other countries; from croissants and brioches to bagels and rye cobs. There are many popular ones from around the globe and I have included some of these recipes in this book.

We even have local bread recipes from various regions in the British Isles, many with their own histories and stories attached and some with recipes zealously protected by the local people as an integral part of their own regonal heritage.

Chapter Two
Simply the Best

I will not make up a wonderful, romantic story about how I always ate homemade bread as a child. This was certainly not the case, but we did always eat bread made in the small local bakery on our high street and it was very good. Making bread wasn't something my Mum ever did when I was young. She was a wonderful cook and she became famous for the pies she baked with her hand made pastry, but as far as bread making is concerned I introduced my Mum to the glories of baking this staple

When I was at high school, the highlight of my week was Thursday afternoon. We had a triple lesson of what was then called 'Domestic Science' taught by a lovely lady called Miss Braddock. She had her very grey hair tied back in a neat bun and the gentlest of dispositions which enabled her to scold with the merest whisper. I was entranced by her enthusiasm for cooking everything from jam tarts to shepherd's pie but one week, at the end of a lesson, Miss Braddock told us what we would be making in the next lesson. It was going to be bread or, as Miss B. said, 'You will be experiencing how to make your very own loaf of bread.'

Whilst it sounded exciting, little did I know what a great pleasure it was and still is. I always get a tingle of pleasure seeing my new bread emerge from the oven and even now I still ask if it's OK - not so much because I'm worried about it but because I love hearing how much the family likes it.

I still buy bread from various bakers and sometimes from supermarkets. There are some excellent branded loaves, usually the seeded or multi-grained breads and my family love what is known as 'tiger bread' which can be purchased from most supermarkets. It is not always convenient to make your own and I wholeheartedly believe that it should never be seen as a chore but rather as a pleasure. Eating other people's bread has the added advantage of giving you further ideas for new flavours or shapes of loaves and also helps confirm just how easily this remarkable product can be made at home.

I am constantly learning about varieties of bread, the vast array of grains that can be used, the seemingly endless ways of cooking the dough and how you can use the finished product in other dishes.
The main reason for making your own bread is

health and the fact that you will know exactly what has gone into it. Knowledge of ingredients has become ever more important in recent years, especially when you consider the additives that can be used legally in foodstuffs sold in shops.

Reading down the list of ingredients used in a well-known brand of ordinary sliced white loaf there were four E numbers listed. Two were harmless emulsifiers and a preserver which inhibits mould growth, but one caused alarm. E920, L-Cysteine, is a flour 'improver' that creates a more stretchy dough, making bread lighter and more full of holes. It sells you air rather than bread so, in other words, it means the bread is made cheaper to make by using this ingredient.

You can alter the amount of salt in homemade bread to suit your personal taste and dietary requirements. Knowing the salt content in shop bought bread is useful and it is usually printed on the label, although some shop brand loafs don't do this as they can conceal any ingredient which may be a constituent part of another ingredient.

A basic recipe for a loaf of plain, home-baked bread only requires four ingredients, so seeing a chart listing ten or twelve ingredients on a loaf of bread seems a little ridiculous but this is why a mass-produced loaf tastes so different from a homemade one.

In addition, baking your own bread is an excellent stress reliever and very good for you. Pummelling and pulling the dough takes quite a substantial amount of energy and if, you feel so inclined, you can imagine the dough is whoever has last angered you [although of course I have never done this!].

Now regarded as a rural classic, William Cobbett wrote in 'Cottage Economy' (1823) 'Let a woman bake a bushel once a week and she will do very well without phials and gallipots.' [Phials and gallipots were medicines and potions to cure illnesses]. I don't know how true this idea for keeping one healthy is but I do know the more often I bake my own bread the better I feel and it certainly beats the gym for strengthening your hands and arm muscles. It also gives you a feeling of contentment knowing the bread is made by your own hand and that it is something others will enjoy.

Finally, baking bread at home has never been easier than it is today. The yeast ingredients are particularly easy to use [this is explained in depth in Chapter 2] and there is ever more variety to choose from. There is also a wider choice of flours available to us, from strong white to granary and all the variations in between and the quality is more consistent than it was a generation ago. There is a quite horrific story in Mancunian folklore about a local miller adding ground human bones to his flour as he worked close to the Manchester plague pit, an un-flagged grave containing many bodies. He was supposedly seen digging up skeletons at night and taking them back to his mill. This may just be a story to entertain or scare people, but the addition of chalk to flour was indeed proven true. This was done to whiten the flour and keep the cost down. Quality control these days would, of course, never allow additions such as this.

Most supermarkets stock various flours and makes and a few actually have their own brand of bread flour in white, brown and wholemeal ranges.

Utensils have also never been better. Whereas you may use simple multi-purpose baking tins and sheets, there are also some very high tech ones which make the job both easier and more successful. [Read more about this in Chapter 3]

Baking your own bread is a sensual experience. You rely on your sense of touch when making the dough and can feel it change as you mix and knead it. Whilst the bread is cooking you can also smell the aroma, which many people describe as one of their all time favourites and of course you will see and taste the finished product. So that's already four senses engaged in the process!

As if all this wasn't enough to tempt you to have a go at home bread making, one of the main reasons for doing it for me is the feeling of accomplishment and pride as you lift the bread out of the oven. The added bonus, though, is hearing the continuous compliments your family and friends bestow on you every time they taste it. A close friend came to visit just after I had finished baking a batch of loaves. He was amazed and said it was very impressive seeing all the bread piled up on the cooling tray.

Bread making doesn't have to be complicated. As a starting point, a basic white loaf recipe can give you the same feeling of contentment as making one of the more advanced types of bread.

Chapter Three
Looking at Ingredients.

This can be both the easiest and yet the most complicated part of making your own bread as the simplest recipe contains only four ingredients; flour, yeast, salt and water. To vary your bread making and eating experience, however, there are many different flours and other ingredients you may add to the mixture..

If we are going to look at the various ingredients used in bread making, the best place to begin is with flour in its many forms. The wheat grain is composed of three parts: bran, germ and the endosperm. The object of milling grains is to separate the endosperm from the bran and the germ. This produces the popular white flour. The different types of flour contain the other two components in varying degrees.

Shops now sell a wide range of bagged flours for making bread. There are various mixes of grains and textures of wheat flours which provide a wide variety for easy bread making. However, they are quite expensive and can make home baking cost more than shop bought bread but purchasing the basic strong white, brown and wholemeal flours plus any other grains separately can bring the cost down considerably.

Wheat Flour

To make bread it is best to use a strong flour as this produces the best overall loaf. Its high gluten content makes the dough elastic and gives the finished loaf its substance, volume and texture. All wheat flours suitable for making bread will say 'strong plain flour' on the packet. Wheat flour is what most commercially baked bread is made from and other grain based flours may be added to it to vary the texture and flavour. I have used ordinary plain flour to bake bread if ever I have run out of strong but don't leave this bread to prove for as long as the diminished gluten content will affect the finished result - it could flop over.

White
This is probably the most popular flour to begin

with, as it is easiest to handle.

Wholemeal
This contains the whole grain, including the bran.

Wheatmeal
This is similar to wholemeal but with some of the coarser bran removed.

Brown
Contains 10-15% less bran than wholemeal.

Soft Grain
Uses white flour with added kibbled wheat or rye grains.

Country Malted
Has malted wheat flakes added to give a nutty flavour and an interesting texture.

Granary
With malted whole grains added to wholemeal.

Rye Flour
This can be made into bread but it has a low gluten content so it is often mixed with wheat flour. The more rye flour used, the denser and more crumbly the texture of the finished bread. Rye is the main ingredient in the dark German pumpernickel bread.

Buckwheat
This flour is unsuitable for making bread. It isn't actually wheat and has no gluten in the flour. It makes very good pancakes, Russian blinis and

French gallettes.

Oatmeal
This is a wonderful ingredient in bread as it adds flavour, texture and nutritional value. However, it cannot be used as the only grain to make bread due to the lack of gluten.

Cornmeal or Maize
This can be ground into flour to make bread. A typical recipe would still use a half quantity of wheat flour. Cornbread is very popular in the United States as are corn fritters. Cornmeal or polenta may be added to bread recipes to give texture to the finished loaf.

Cornflour
This is used to lighten shortbread and cakes and to thicken sauces.

Soya Flour
This cannot be used on its own to make bread as it is gluten free, but due to its high protein content (almost twice as much as wheat flour) makes a good addition to the ingredients list. A recipe shouldn't, however, contain more than 10- 20% soya flour as the final result would become heavy and inedible.

Gram flour
This flour is made from ground chickpeas and is gluten free. It is used in Asian cookery to make pakoras and bhajis. In Italy gram flour is used to make crisp pizza like pancakes called Farinata. The flour is mixed with water and olive oil, then cooked on a griddle. The French call the flour Socca and it

The Bread and Butter Book

is used in the Nice region to make a thick porridge which when cold may be sliced, fried and served with sugar.

Rice Flour
This is often used to make pastries in Asian cookery but is not generally used in bread making.

Potato Flour
This is almost pure starch and is used as a thickening agent in dishes but potatoes can make delicious breads and flat breads, (see recipe section).

Raising Agents

Flour is the main ingredient in any bread recipe, but most doughs require a raising agent to produce the correct texture and popular finished product.

The most widely used of these is yeast, but baking soda or baking powder is also used to make a loaf. Buttermilk is often used in conjunction with baking soda as its acidity helps to boost the rising of the dough in both soda breads and scones.

Yeast
Yeast can be bought in various forms, some easier to use than others, but most giving the same overall finished product.

Yeast is alive when used in baking and needs certain conditions to fulfil its job properly. The job of the yeast is to cause the dough to rise which it does because of the gas produced by the yeast and released in certain conditions. It it requires warmth, food and liquid. The liquid is either milk, water or a combination of both. The liquid is heated but not hot or boiling as this would kill the yeast and therefore stop it working in the dough. A small amount of sugar is mixed with the yeast to provide the food. When these conditions prevail the yeast can then get to work.

The gas produced that causes the dough to rise is carbon dioxide which comes from a breakdown of sugar to release energy. The energy produced makes more yeast in the dough as it reproduces. The carbon dioxide is simply a waste product which the yeast then ejects, allowing the bread to rise.

Yeast for baking is either fresh or dried.

Fresh Yeast
This is sold in a compressed block and is a fawn/ beige colour. It is sold by weight and a piece cut for use from the main block. It should look moist with a fresh aroma. If the yeast looks dry or darker in colour in places and smells acidic it should not be used as it may be contaminated. If required fresh yeast may be stored in the fridge for several days and can be frozen successfully. If it is frozen it must be thoroughly thawed at room temperature before it is used in baking. It must be combined with a little warm water and a pinch of sugar and left in a warm place until the mixture is frothy. This shows that the yeast is working and can be used in recipes.

Dried yeast comes in three basic forms.

The Bread and Butter Book

Standard Dried Yeast

This is granulated and needs to be reconstituted before use. Mixing it with warm water and a little sugar does this. The manufacturer will recommend quantities. This can then be used as fresh yeast.

Easy-blend Dried Yeast

This is fine granules of yeast that may be added straight to the dry ingredients in the bread recipe. The liquid required is then added to both the yeast and the other dry ingredients together.

Fast-action Easy-blend Dried Yeast

This is also in the form of fine granules and is added to the dry ingredients at the beginning of the recipe. The reason it is called fast-action is that it speeds up the rising of the dough so only one period of proving is necessary before cooking. The ingredient added to the yeast which enables this speedier action is ascorbic acid or vitamin C.

The latter is the most widely available of yeast types and I have found it the easiest to use for everyday bread making. But using the Easy-blend dried yeast is also very easy and can give a better result as the dough requires two proving times, making a lighter finished product. I very rarely use fresh yeast as it is so difficult to obtain, but it is good to have a go at baking your bread with it. I enjoy watching how the yeast works in the warm liquid as it bubbles and shows that it is ready to be added to the flour. On the whole, though, fast-action yeast has proved how easy it is to make your own bread and is the most popular form of yeast in use today.

Looking at Ingredients

Bread can be made without using yeast as its raising agent. For instance bicarbonate of soda is a leavening agent which is used in Soda bread. Soda bread originates in Ireland and was traditionally cooked in a covered pot over an open fire. The soda is activated by the addition of an acidic liquid such as buttermilk. It starts to produce carbon-dioxide in the mixture, causing the dough to rise as soon as the liquid is added to the flour and soda. It is therefore a fast raising agent. Proving isn't necessary as it rises as it cooks rather like a cake would. It is a very quick way to make a loaf of bread, but it doesn't keep fresh for as long as a yeast based mixtures. It really is better eaten whilst still warm or on the same day as baking.

Not all bread recipes call for the mixture to use a raising agent. There are many recipes for flat breads from throughout the world included in the recipe section.

Salt

We have covered two of the main ingredients in bread making; the flour and the raising agent. The next important addition is salt. Without this the bread would taste very odd.

When I was young my Mum regularly bought her bread from our local baker at the bottom of our road. The bread was baked in the back of the shop by a couple called George and Katie and, after baking the bread, they would then serve the customers at opening time. Often I would go with my Mum as the shop opened at about 7.45am. Then we would go home and have fresh bread for breakfast before I went to school. Many families in the surrounding area would do this so much of the available bread was already sold by 8.30am. One morning we got home and sat down to our meal of warm bread and butter. It was revolting and Mum ran back to the shop together with many other people following. George and Katie had forgotten to add the salt to their dough, so a whole batch of bread was wasted. At that time any waste food was sent to the local pig farmer. I remember being late for school alongside many others because of this catastrophe. After that the locals never let them forget the salt again, always asking 'Is there salt in this lot?'

Salt is always added to the flour and mixed in before the yeast is incorporated as salt slows the reaction of the yeast and stops it working as efficiently. But it is diluted enough when added to the flour for this not to be a problem in making bread.

Liquid

The liquid used to make bread may be water, milk or a combination of both. Some dessert bread recipes call for other liquids like fruit juices. This is always warm in yeast cookery as it requires heat to begin doing its job. It must not, however, be too hot as this would kill the yeast. The ideal temperature is warm to the touch, so always dip in a finger to test it before adding it to the rest of the ingredients.

Fat

If made with these four ingredients your bread will taste good and keep for a day or so, but no longer. For bread to remain fresh for longer one needs to add some fat or oil to the mixture.

This can be butter, lard or margarine which is rubbed into the flour before adding the yeast. However, I tend to use oil as it is simply added to the dough with the liquid. Butter may be melted gently over a very low heat to be added in a similar way to oil. This is often called for in sweetened doughs as it gives a rich, creamy flavour and a softer finished product.

Any good quality oil will do, the choice depends entirely on your own taste. I tend to use either rapeseed, sunflower or olive oil. Extra virgin oil gives a particularly good flavour to bread and is often used to make Italian Foccacia.

Other highly flavoured oils like sesame or walnut should be added carefully and should be used in conjunction with a flavourless oil or the taste would be too overpowering and spoil the bread.

Optional extras

Other additions to bread are the many seeds, herbs, nuts and grains that change the flavour and texture of the bread. They may be added to white, brown or wholemeal flours during the preparation of the dough and make a tasty alternative to a plain loaf,

Seeds	Herbs	Nuts	Grains
Sunflower	Parsley	Use un-	Barley
Sesame	Thyme	salted	Oats
Poppy	Rosemary	and chop	Toasted
Pumpkin	Sage	before use	wheat
Caraway	Chives	Peanut	Rye
Linseed	Tarragon	Walnut	
Fennel	Dill	Hazelnut	
Coriander	Marjoram	Almond	
Cumin		Cashew	
Onion		Pecan	

In sweetened dough dried fruits such as raisins, sultanas, candied peels, currants, cranberries, apples, prunes, pineapple, mangoes, cherries, pears, figs and dates are often added.

In savoury breads you can add such ingredients as sun-dried tomatoes, olives, peppers, caramelised onions and cheese.

In dessert breads an egg is often used to enrich the dough. This gives the finished bread a creamy taste and the soft texture most associated with sweetened breads.

Vitamin C is regularly added to the yeast to improve its efficiency and the speed at which it begins to work within the dough. It also strengthens the gluten in the wheat so you get a better end product that is lighter and more uniformly risen. This is why you will find the word 'IMPROVER' in the list of ingredients on a commercially produced loaf. It is simply vitamin C.

In the past rosehip syrup was added to the yeast as the combined sugar and vitamin C content helped kick-start the yeast into action.

In soda bread cookery the softness and light texture is achieved by adding an acidic ingredient to the flour and soda mixture. This is usually in the form of the liquid ingredient in the recipe, the milk. Buttermilk is naturally acidic and is often used in making a soda loaf, but adding a tablespoon of lemon juice to ordinary milk works equally well. If you find yourself with some milk that has just turned sour, don't waste it. Use at least some of it in baking soda bread. Souring milk is also acidic and makes excellent bread and scones, but do make sure it isn't too far gone or too solid.

This book has many different recipes for you to try. The quantities and variety of ingredients will enable you to experiment and find your own personal favourites. I have no doubt forgotten some and you will no doubt discover more. Bread recipes can easily be changed or adapted very successfully.

The next part of this chapter looks at the basic utensils you will need to make your bread. Some are for more specific baking needs so there is no need to rush out and buy everything mentioned in the following pages.

Necessary Utensils.

Bread needs to be baked at a high temperature to kill the yeast, so an oven that reaches at least 225°C/

gas mark 8 is a must. Bread bakes equally well in all types of ovens and we have just acquired a small brick and clay oven in our garden which makes great bread and has that authentic edge to it.

Mixing the Dough.

A large mixing bowl is needed even if you only make a small quantity of dough, as it is much easier to work with and keeps the heat of the mixture fairly constant, helping with the proving of the dough. I use a plastic bowl to make my bread as I find ceramic ones are too heavy for me to carry around the kitchen when full of dough, but they are better at insulating the mixture than a plastic or metal bowl. Metal bowls are the least effective at keeping the dough warm so don't use them for bread making.

I prefer to mix the dry and liquid ingredients together with a large wooden spoon before getting my hands in. You can also use a metal spoon but I find a wooden one easier and quicker to use.

Depending on the shape of the bread you want to make you will need a good quality baking tray or several if you wish to make small rolls. Non-stick bakeware isn't necessary, I use one of each and both work equally well so long as they are lightly oiled before the dough is placed on them. Baking trays are needed to make small or large sized cobs and loaves, but to make a traditional shaped loaf you will need a loaf tin. These can be made of steel with or without a non-stick coating but I have found an invaluable one made of silicone. This never needs oiling and is totally non-stick but because it is pliable and wobbly, I find it easier to handle if you place the container on a baking sheet before it goes in the oven rather than straight onto the oven rack. If you want perfectly formed small rolls this can be done by using a muffin tin. The shapes make perfect little cobs which are very cute and guaranteed to impress your dinner guests.

Cooling racks are a must as the bread needs the air to circulate around it or the crust will lose its crispness and becomes soggy. This is due to the moisture exuding from the bread while it is hot. Once it is cool this stops and the bread can then be kept in a covered container like any other bread.

Terracotta makes an excellent container for cooking bread and the various size plant pots are often used to make unusual shaped loaves. They need oiling well as the dough really sticks to the sides which can spoil the shape of the finished product. I have actually bought some pots in varying sizes for this job as the loaf slices in an interesting shape and looks good on the plate. Earthenware pots and dishes are very versatile as they can be used for a wide variety of recipes, not just for bread making.

To make tortilla and chapati style bread you will need a heavy based, good quality, flat bottomed frying pan or griddle. The pan needs to get very hot and remain so till all the pieces of bread are cooked, so the best quality pan you can afford will stand you in good stead for all sorts of recipes.

Chapter Four
Techniques

Bread making, just like any other form of cookery, is a combination of both science and art. The science is how the ingredients work together during preparation and cooking. The art is understanding the ingredients, judging when you have to tweak a recipe and how the finished product is viewed.

So knowing the techniques involved in making bread and why they are used helps us to understand the way bread is successfully made.

The ingredient that fascinates and sometimes alarms people the most is the yeast. This is probably because it needs precise conditions to do its job successfully. A little knowledge about yeast should help to subdue any worries about using it.

As I have already explained yeast requires warmth, food and moisture to reproduce. A warm kitchen is therefore required when baking bread and all the dry ingredients must be at room temperature. The food for yeast is always sugar in some form or other and the liquid added to the dough provides the moisture. These three simple conditions allow the yeast to thrive and in doing so will work the miracle of producing a soft well risen loaf of bread. The yeast will simply produce carbon dioxide as it respires, so the dough rises and produces the effect we are expecting.

Steps to Making a Successful Loaf

If you are using fresh or ordinary dried yeast then begin by making a ferment mixture which will consist of the yeast, the warm liquid from the recipe and a teaspoon of sugar. Stir this well and leave it in a warm place for 20-30 minutes until it is frothy.

The basic method for bread making is very simple. Sift the flour and salt together into a warm mixing bowl and rub in the fat if using it in the recipe. Add the ferment mixture and combine well with a wooden spoon.

The next step isto knead the dough. This is an important stage in bread making as it determines the outcome of the finished loaf. Some people like a firm, dense texture to their bread and so do very little kneading of the dough. Most people, on the other hand, prefer a softer, lighter dough, therefore a good kneading is essential.

Kneading is mostly done by hand although it can be be done with a mixer and dough hooks. These are very useful for anyone with arthritis in their hands or any other debilitating problem. The dough does require the kneading process as this action develops the gluten in the flour and produces soft, springy bread that will hold its shape.

The action of kneading is simple enough and you will get used to it the more you do it. I prefer to do it in the mixing bowl as it keeps the dough warm and helps with the shape, but most people knead the dough on a lightly floured kitchen surface. Try both ways and see which is easier for you.

Hold the dough steady with one hand and pull at it with the other. Pull at the edge and stretch it away from you, then fold it back over the bulk of the dough. Repeat this action constantly for 10 minutes. Any less time and the bread won't be as soft and light. Correctly kneaded, the dough has a smooth appearance. It should look firm and have an elastic texture. If you gently prod it with your finger to form a 'dimple' it should recover quickly.

Wholemeal or granary flour may need a longer kneading time. It is very difficult to over knead by hand, but it may happen if you use a machine and this can cause a problem with the bread holding its shape. Over kneading can loosen the elasticity and spoil the finished product. So, if you are using a machine, take care with the length of time the dough is kneaded. Always follow the manufacturer's instructions and use a slow speed on the machine, at least until you are thoroughly familiar with the process.

If you are using fresh or ordinary dried yeast, the next step is the first proving time. This is to allow the yeast time to work and to give a well-risen and even dough. After you have kneaded your dough, place it (or leave it) in a warm bowl and cover it with a clean tea cloth. Place the bowl in a warm area until the dough has doubled in size. This requirement has troubled many people who have sought out space in an airing cupboard or the like. In actual fact a well-kneaded dough with the right ingredients will rise in most places of average temperature.

After this time has elapsed the dough must be 'knocked back.' This gets rid of any uneven pockets of air in the dough and restores the texture of the mixture. To 'knock back' simply take the dough out of the bowl, place it on the work surface and punch into the dough with your fist. It should not require much flour as it won't be sticky and too much extra flour will make the bread streaky. This is good for getting rid of any aggressive feelings you may be harbouring and it is also very good for the bread. Knead it quickly for a few seconds till it has regained its shape.

The next stage is the shaping of the dough. There are many traditional shapes of loaves that are fun to try and various sizes and shapes of tin. This is purely a matter of preference and choice but it is good to vary the shape of your bread depending on what you want to use the bread for once it is baked.

The Bread and Butter Book

Sandwiches are best made with bread baked in tins as it gives a more regular shape and homemade burgers are best eaten with flat type bread rolls.

The basic traditional shapes are:

The Bloomer

This is a long cob with diagonal cuts along the top of the bread. They can be any size to suit your taste and needs and are very easy to produce. It is good for slicing and large ones make reasonable shaped sandwiches.

The Cottage Loaf

The dough is cut into two sections, one containing about two thirds of the dough. These two pieces are shaped into round balls and the base of the smaller section is moistened with water and placed on top of the larger ball. Then, using your index and middle fingers, push down through the centre of the smaller top section through to the larger base. This will keep the two pieces together.

The Plait

Bread can be shaped into a three strand or a five strand plait. The latter makes a larger loaf sized plait that's good for slicing and the three strander is better for the smaller, single roll. Divide small sections of dough into threes and roll  each section into thin sausage shapes. Squeeze three ends of the strands together and seal them with a little water. Plait the strands loosely and finally squeeze and moisten the other ends together in the same way as before.

The five strander is a little more complicated. Divide the dough into five larger sausage shapes, moisten and squeeze the ends together and then spread the strands slightly apart. Number the stands 1-5 and follow this pattern, renumbering the strands as you go along; 2 over 3, 5 over 2, 1 over 3. Continue  the sequence till you reach the end of the strands. Moisten and squeeze together to seal the other ends as before.

This might sound complicated but the finished result is very impressive and gives an interesting shape to the sliced loaf.

37

The Tin Loaf

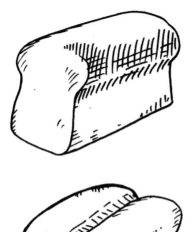

The traditional tin loaf is by far the easiest option. Shaping is very simple as when the dough rises it takes on the shape of whatever you have put it in. As long as they are well greased most baking tins make good containers for bread. Mould the amount of dough required for the tin, remembering that it will almost double in size during the proving time. Place it in the centre of the tin and leave it. It will mould itself as it rises.

A Split tin loaf is made by making a deep cut in the top of the dough about 15-20 minutes into the proving time, then leaving it to finish rising before baking.

Individual Rolls

These are ideal for dinner parties, picnics, lunch boxes or to serve with soup or hors d'oeuvres. They can be round rolls or bridge rolls, which are more elongated in shape. Break off small amounts of dough and knead them into either a round or a sausage shape which tapers towards the ends. If you want to make your own burger buns, break off the required amount and form a round. As you place it on the baking sheet gently flatten it with the palm of your hand. The finished item will be a little flatter and ready to take a burger.

The Scroll

This is an interesting one. It is used as a fancy bread for special occasions and is a bit tricky to make, but looks good as a centre piece at a buffet party. The dough is rolled out fairly thickly into a basic triangle shape, then rolled from the wide end to the narrow tip giving a scroll effect. It is then left to prove for 15 minutes, brushed with egg and milk glaze, left for a further 10 minutes and then cooked.

Another way of making the scroll shape is to roll the dough into a rectangle and roll from one end half way then turn the dough over and roll from the other end making an 's' shape. This is then left to prove like the first example and finished in the same way.

At Harvest time celebrations a traditional 'Wheatsheaf' is made out of dough. This is a large, ornate, flat loaf in the shape of a sheaf of wheat that is often used as the centre of a harvest display. It is usually made by the local professional baker.

The Bread and Butter Book

If you use fast acting yeast and only one proving is necessary, now is the time to leave your bread to prove and rise until it doubles in size. Once shaped it needs a warm place to rise before baking. Fast action yeast speeds up the proving time, so watch your dough. Don't just assume the time given in a recipe is correct. These are only guides and over-proving the dough has certainly spoiled many loaves which can lose their shape and often tilt over.

Finishing a loaf comes generally just before or even during baking. This affects the finished crust. You can sprinkle the top with various seeds such as sesame, poppy or sunflower seeds and gently press them into the top of the loaf. This will give a crunchy topping to the bread. Oatmeal also gives an interesting finish to a loaf but isn't quite as crunchy for those who prefer a softer finish.

For a soft crust dust the dough with flour or brush it with vegetable oil and for a crispy crust brush the top of the bread with a salt-water mixture using ½ a teaspoon of salt to 4 tablespoons of hot water. Allow the mixture to cool before brushing it over the top of the dough.

Brushing with a teaspoon of sugar mixed with two tablespoons of milk will give a brown, crusty finish and egg and milk together will produce a shiny glaze on top of the finished loaf. Mix one egg with three tablespoons of milk and brush generously over the dough before cooking. This mixture will keep overnight in a refrigerator.

Baking the dough has two main purposes. The

first and most obvious one is the cooking of the ingredients to make the bread edible. The second, and equally important purpose, is the killing of the yeast. Having your oven set to a high temperature does the latter. As yeast is very sensitive to high temperatures it is killed in the first few minutes of cooking, so some recipes may ask you to turn down the heat after a while so that the bread is not over cooked. Most recipes, however, use a continuous high heat suitable for the size and type of loaf.

Testing if a loaf is cooked is usually down to the look and sound of the loaf. This may sound odd but the sound you get from a cooked loaf is a very definite thudding sound when tapped on the bottom of the loaf. If the loaf is in a tin it will need to be removed to do this. Use oven gloves at all times as the bread will be incredibly hot. Turn the loaf over and tap the base with the palm of your hand. If it is cooked through it will produce a hollow, thudding sound.

The loaf should also be dark and golden in colour and, if cooked in a tin, should be slightly shrunken away from the sides. If the top of the loaf is cooking too quickly it may be in the wrong place in your oven, so alter its position by placing it on a lower shelf or turn the temperature down by a few degrees. When the bread is cooked, take it out of the tin or off the baking tray straight away and place it on a cooling tray as the crust will go soggy from the moisture emanating from the loaf. Cooling is a very important part of baking bread and, whereas small rolls are OK to be eaten warm, slicing too soon may actually spoil a larger loaf. Leave it to cool for at least 45 minutes before eating as slicing a hot

The Bread and Butter Book

loaf will squash its shape and the bread will lose its springy texture.

To recap, the basic stages in bread making are, if you use fresh or ordinary dried yeast:

1.Mixing
2.Kneading
3.Proving
4.Knocking back
5.Shaping
6.Proving
7.Finishing
8.Baking
9.Cooling

The basic stages for when you use fast action yeast are:

1.Mixing
2.Kneading
3.Shaping
4.Proving
5.Finishing
6.Baking
7.Cooling

42

Chapter Five
Family Bread Recipes

The majority of these recipes are the traditional everyday loaves that are consumed daily in most households. I've tried to include all the basic recipes using each variety of yeast and the many flour types that are now readily available. Some are easy but others are a little more complicated and these may require a little experience. The first recipe is the quickest and easiest type of bread to make and is ideal when you want fresh bread fast. It contains no yeast so there is no proving or kneading necessary.

Soda Bread

This bread tastes wonderful a few minutes after baking and, unlike yeasted bread, will not give you indigestion so soon after baking because of its soda content. I usually serve this with homemade soups or cheese and pickles for lunch. It isn't possible to make a conventional sandwich with it because of its crumbly texture but, once cool, it is ideal for an open sandwich. Soda bread needs to be eaten on the same day as it is baked, but this shouldn't be a problem once you have tasted it. In our house it rarely cools before being gobbled up. This recipe requires buttermilk, which can be bought in a carton from the supermarket, or you can make your own as described in the final chapter.

30 minute Soda Bread

450g/1lb self-raising flour
Level teaspoon salt
Level teaspoon baking powder
284ml/10fl oz carton buttermilk or
280ml/10fl oz of home made buttermilk

Preheat the oven to 220°C/Gas mark 7 and grease a baking tray with a little oil. Sift the flour, salt and baking powder together in a large mixing bowl. Stir in the buttermilk and bind to a soft dough. The mixture should be a little sticky. If the mixture seems dry add a little more milk or water.

Form into a round and place on a baking tray. Cut diagonally across the top of the loaf, making four sections. Bake for 20-25 minutes until golden brown.

Oaty Soda Bread

This is my personal favourite as it has the addition of health giving oats. Use 350g/12oz flour and 100g/4oz medium rolled oats. Other ingredients are the same as above, but in the method stir in the oats after sifting the flour, salt and baking powder together. Finish as in the basic recipe.

Cheese Soda Bread

After mixing all the dry ingredients, add 50g/2oz of mature cheddar cheese to the mixture before adding the buttermilk. Continue as in the basic method.

You may also add fresh or dried herbs to the mixture. I like to add half a teaspoon of dried thyme or a teaspoon of fresh thyme to the recipe before mixing in the liquid ingredient.

Chopped, sun-dried tomatoes or olives are another delicious addition, but do be careful to drain all the oil or brine from the ones that come in a jar.

Simple White Loaf

This recipe is the least complicated bread to make using yeast and will make two medium sized loaves.

900g/2lb strong white flour
2 level teaspoons salt
1 sachet fast action dried yeast
1 tablespoon sunflower oil
450ml/³/₄ pint to 568ml/1pint warm water

Sieve the flour and salt into a large bowl and stir in the yeast. Make a well in centre of the flour and add the oil and water, mixing well with a wooden spoon. Use your hands to finish combining the flour and water and begin kneading in the bowl. Transfer the dough, if you wish, to a lightly floured surface and knead for 10 minutes. Alternatively, keep kneading in the bowl.
Shape the dough into your preferred shape and place in oiled tins or baking trays and leave to prove till doubled in size. This will take approximately 35-45 minutes in a warm place. Bake at 220°C/Gas mark 7 for 30- 40 minutes.

White Bread using Fresh or Dried Yeast
(makes 3 medium sized loaves)

1.4kg/3lb strong white flour
4 level teaspoons salt
25g/1oz fresh yeast or
15g/¹/₂oz dried yeast

2 teaspoons sugar
2 tablespoons sunflower oil
1 tablespoon sugar
900ml/1½ pints warm water

Crumble the fresh yeast into the warm water or stir or mix the dried yeast with 450ml/¾ pint of warm water. Add the 2 teaspoons of sugar. Leave for 15 minutes in a warm place until frothy. Sieve the flour and salt together in a large bowl and make a well in the centre. Add the yeast mixture, the extra water if using dried yeast, the oil and the sugar. Mix well with a wooden spoon, then finish combining the ingredients by hand.

Knead till the mixture forms a smooth ball, transfering to a lightly floured surface and kneading for a further 10 minutes.

Place the dough in a very lightly oiled bowl, cover with a clean tea-towel and leave to prove till the dough has doubled in size.

Knock back the dough and knead for a further 5 minutes. Shape the dough into the desired shape and place in or on oiled cooking utensils and leave to prove again till doubled in size. Bake at 220°C/Gas mark 7 for 30- 40 minutes.

Granary Bread

The last two recipes can be made with brown, wholemeal or a mixture of white and wholemeal or brown, substituting amounts as necessary. Wholemeal flour needs a little more liquid than white flour so you will need to adjustthe amounts of liquid, adding about 20ml extra if using wholemeal on its own.

Granary flour is now widely available and makes a tasty filling bread. It gives a very nutty flavour to the loaf.

Quick Granary Loaf

450g/1lb white strong flour
450g/1lb granary flour
1 sachet fast action dried yeast
568ml/1pint warm water but a little more may be required depending on the flour
1 tablespoon sunflower oil
2 level teaspoons salt

Method as for Simple White loaf, mixing the flours together at the beginning of the recipe.

Milk Bread

Milk bread is a great alternative to ordinary white bread. It is very soft but makes wonderfully crispy toast. The following recipe is sufficient for one loaf.

Milk Loaf

450g/1lb strong white flour
1 level teaspoon salt
1 sachet fast action dried yeast
275ml/ ½ pint warm whole milk

Sieve the flour and salt into a large bowl and stir in the yeast, making a well in the centre of the flour. Gradually stir in the warm milk and combine by hand into a ball, kneading for 10 minutes till smooth. Shape into a large roll. Place on an oiled baking sheet and leave to prove till doubled in size.

Bake for 30-35 minutes at 220°C/Gas mark 7.

Using Oatmeal

This is one of my family's favourites. The oats gives an added nutty taste and have significant health benefits too.

Oatmeal Bread

700g/1½lbs strong white flour
200g/8oz fine oatmeal
1 sachet fast action dried yeast
2 teaspoons salt
450ml/¾pint to 568ml/1pint warm water
1 tablespoon sunflower oil

Sieve the flour and salt into a bowl and stir in the oats and yeast. Make a well in the centre, add the water and oil and stir. Use your hands to combine the ingredients and form into a ball. Knead for 10 minutes until smooth.

Divide the mixture into two and form into rounds. Leave to prove till doubled in size.

Bake for 25-30 minutes at 220°C/Gas mark 7.

Old-Fashioned Herb Bread

This loaf has a very different texture to other breads. It is very soft and has an open texture that makes it ideal served with patés and soft cheese. You can use whichever herbs you prefer or a grand mixture so that each mouthful may taste slightly different. Good herb mixtures are tarragon and parsley or marjoram and thyme and sage and chives gives a good savoury flavour. if you use these herbs only add 1 tablespoon of fresh and 1 teaspoon of dried.

350g/12oz strong white flour
1 large, beaten egg
1 tablespoon sunflower oil
1/2 sachet fast action dried yeast
225ml/8fl oz warm milk
1 1/2 teaspoons salt
2 tablespoons finely chopped fresh herbs or 1 1/2 teaspoons dried herbs of your choice
Fennel or poppy seeds for sprinkling on top

Sieve the salt and flour together into a bowl and stir in the yeast. Combine the egg and milk in a jug and pour into the centre of the flour, leaving a little to brush the top of the loaf before baking.
Add the oil and herbs you are using and mix well with a wooden spoon. Add a little more flour if the mixture is too sticky, but only teaspoon by teaspoon so that you don't add too much. Use your hands to combine the ingredients into

a ball and knead for 10 minutes.

Shape so that the dough fits into an oiled 2lb loaf tin and leave to prove until either doubled in size or standing slightly proud of the tin.

Gently brush the top with the leftover egg and milk mixture and sprinkle your loaf with your choice of seeds.

Bake for 30-35 minutes at 210°C/Gas mark 6. Use two 1lb tins if you want a smaller loaf for serving with paté as a starter and bake for 5-10 minutes less than previously.

Potato Bread

Potato bread is filling and nutritious. It makes a real treat on those cold winter days, especially when eaten with warming soups. This recipe makes one large loaf or two smaller cobs. If using a tin this corresponds to a 2lb or two 1lb tins.

1 medium sized potato, weighing about 5-6oz
500g/1lb 2oz strong white flour
2 teaspoons salt
250ml/8fl oz warm milk
1 egg
1 sachet fast action dried yeast
3 tablespoons crème fraiche

Grate the raw potato into a large bowl. Pour over the warm milk and add the yeast. Sieve the flour and salt together in a separate bowl and gradually beat half the flour into the potato mixture. Beat in the egg and crème fraiche and follow with the rest of the flour. Knead the dough for 10 minutes and shape. Place in oiled tins or on a baking sheet and prove for 40 minutes. When doubled in size, bake at 180°C/ Gas mark 5 for 45 minutes or 30-35 minutes if smaller loaves have been made.

Onion Bread

Another tasty, savoury bread is made with onions gently fried till they begin to caramelise. I prefer to make this into long flat rolls to be served with soup or salads, or try toasting them with cheese on the top. Delicious.

500g/1lb 2oz strong white flour
2 teaspoons salt
1 sachet fast action dried yeast
280-300ml/½pint warm water
1 tablespoon sunflower oil

For the onion topping:
2 small onions finely sliced
50g/2oz butter
2 level tablespoons plain flour
150ml/5fl oz milk
1 chopped clove garlic (optional)
½ level teaspoon salt
Black pepper to taste
Onion seeds to sprinkle on top

Make the bread as in the simple white bread in the previous recipe, place on a baking tray and flatten well by hand or with a rolling pin. Leave to prove for 30 minutes. Meanwhile, fry the onions gently in the butter, adding the garlic. Continue to cook until the onions begin to caramelise. Sprinkle over the flour and mix well into the onions. Gradually add the milk, stirring all the time and keeping the heat low so the mixture doesn't burn. Bring to the boil then simmer for a few seconds, adding salt and pepper. After the bread has finished proving, spread the onion mixture over the top and sprinkle with the onion seeds. Bake for 25-30 minutes at 200ºC/ Gas mark 6.

Tomato Loaf

This is a very unusual and great flavoured bread and is one that I saw on one of Keith Floyd's television programmes. Over the years I have added different ingredients and have changed the recipe. Have a go at this one but try adding your own favourite ingredients.

750g/1lb 8oz strong white flour
Can of tomatoes, drained and chopped (use the remaining liquid in pasta sauces)
1 tablespoon tomato puree
1 sachet fast action dried yeast
1 level teaspoon salt
1 level tablespoon sugar
1 tablespoon olive oil
80ml/3oz warm water or the warmed tomato liquor

Sieve the flour and salt into a large bowl and stir in the yeast and sugar. Add the warm liquid, tomatoes, oil and tomato puree. Mix well with a wooden spoon then use your hands to finish combining and knead for 10 minutes. Place in a well oiled 2lb loaf tin and prove for 30-35 minutes in a warm place. Bake for 30- 40 minutes at 220°C/Gas mark 7.

Individual Rolls

Individual rolls are great to serve at dinner parties. They don't keep as well as larger loaves but if kept in an airtight container rather than a bread bin they will keep quite well. The following recipe makes approximately 18 rolls. You can vary the batch by making different shapes and finishing them with a variety of seeds such as poppy, onion, sesame or fennel on top of each roll.

700g/1lb 8oz strong white or brown flour
2 teaspoons salt
1 sachet fast action dried yeast
1 tablespoon sunflower oil
450ml/¾ pint warm water

Sieve the salt and flour together into a bowl. Add the yeast and stir well. Pour the water into the centre of the flour and add the oil. Mix with a wooden spoon and use your hands to combine into a ball. Knead for 10 minutes and break the dough into 18 small pieces and shape as required. Place on an oiled baking sheet a few centimetres apart and leave to prove for 30 minutes. Bake for 15-20 minutes at 220°C/Gas mark 7.

Rye Bread

This is a really nutty bread with a deep flavour and a very satisfying texture. The following recipe is one that my Grandma used to make and she would prepare Grandad's packed lunch with this because she said it filled him up for longer. He still came home ravenous, though.

300g/10½oz rye flour
200g/7oz strong white flour
300g/10½ oz oats
3 teaspoons salt
25g/1oz fresh yeast
250mls/8fl oz warm water
1 teaspoon sugar

Crumble the fresh yeast into the water and add the sugar. Mix all the dry ingredients together in a large bowl. Add the yeast mixture and combine with your hands until it forms a ball. Add a little more warm water if the dough feels too stiff. Knead in the bowl for 5 minutes, then transfer to a lightly floured surface and knead for a further 5 minutes. Return to the bowl and cover with a clean tea towel. Leave to prove for 30 minutes. Knock back and knead for a few more minutes. Then shape and place in a lightly oiled 2lb loaf tin and leave to prove for a further 30 minutes. Bake for 25-35 minutes at 200°C/Gas mark 6.

Mixed Seed Bread

You can now buy flours ready mixed with seeds but I prefer to add my own in the quantities my family enjoys. It is easy to find many small packs containing all kinds of seeds and this makes it easy to bake a variety of bread with interesting textures. I have found that even the most hardened white bread eaters enjoy the taste of seeded bread. The next recipe is an easy and quick mixed seeded bread.

Either 400g/14oz strong wholemeal flour and
400g/14oz strong white flour
Or 800g/1lb 7oz strong white flour
2 sachets fast action dried yeast
1 tablespoon sunflower oil
3 teaspoons salt
125g/4$\frac{1}{2}$oz mixed seeds of your choice (try linseed, poppy, pumpkin, sesame or sunflower)
280mls/8fl oz warm water

Mix all the dry ingredients together in a large bowl. Make a well in the centre of the flour and add water and oil. Mix together with a wooden spoon. Use your hands to combine the ingredients and form a ball. Knead for 10 minutes. Shape into a round or oval loaf and place on an oiled baking sheet. Leave in a warm place till it has doubled in size. Extra seeds may be sprinkled on the top of the loaf before baking. Brush the top with a little water before sprinkling on the seeds.
Bake for 25-35 minutes at 220°C/Gas mark 7.

Muesli Bread

This is an excellent bread for eating in the morning for breakfast. It is great toasted with lots of butter. It is best made with unsweetened or low sugar muesli as the flavour is better and it can easily become too sweet.

180g/6oz muesli, either fruited or with fruit and nuts
900g/1½lbs strong white flour
1 sachet fast action dried yeast
50g/2oz raisins
50g/2oz melted butter
450ml/¾ pint warm water
1 teaspoon salt

Sieve the flour and salt and stir in the yeast. Add the water and butter and mix well. Knead for 10 minutes and place in 2 well oiled loaf tins. Leave to prove for 40 minutes. Bake for 30-35 minutes at 200°C/ Gas mark 6 until cooked.

Breakfast Muffins

Breakfast muffins and crumpets are a real favourite in our house and are easy to make. You can cook them in a heavy-based frying pan but a griddle pan is best. Crumpets are cooked in the same way as muffins but use a metal ring to keep the mixture in place. Pikelets are made on the griddle without the ring.

275g/10oz strong white flour
2 level teaspoons salt
220ml/8fl oz warm water
½ sachet fast action dried yeast
1 tablespoon sunflower oil

Sieve the flour and salt into a bowl and stir in the yeast. Make a well in the centre of the flour and pour in the water and oil. Combine all the ingredients till a very soft dough is formed. It should still hold its shape, but will be much softer and more difficult to handle than normal dough. Knead the sticky dough for at least 7 minutes and leave to prove in a warm place for 40 minutes. Heat a griddle pan that has been lightly oiled till hot. Break off small sections of the dough and make flat rounds. Cook 3-4 at a time on the griddle, turning down the heat to medium so the crust doesn't burn. Cook for 10-12 minutes, turning the muffin over after 5-6 minutes. Keep each batch warm in the oven until ready to serve. Serve warm with delicious homemade butter (see chapter 11). Tear the muffins apart rather than cutting them with a knife.

Pikelets and Crumpets

I find it better to use fresh yeast in this recipe, as the bubbles form more successfully when the crumpet or pikelet is cooking. There is no kneading to be done but the yeast mixture needs time to ferment to produce the bubbles.

Family Bread Recipes

225g/8oz strong white flour
1 level teaspoon salt
15g/½ oz fresh yeast
½ teaspoon sugar
150ml/¼ pint warm water
150ml/¼ pint warm milk
¼ teaspoon bicarbonate of soda
1 egg white beaten until frothy
4 tablespoons cold water

Sieve the flour and salt together into a large bowl. Mix together the milk and water and crumble in the yeast. Add the sugar and stir. Pour the yeast mixture into the flour and beat vigorously for 5-6 minutes. The batter must be covered and left in a warm place for 30-40 minutes. Dissolve the bicarbonate of soda in the cold water and beat lightly into the batter. Fold in the egg white, making sure it is thoroughly combined into the batter. If cooking pikelets, use a ladle to spoon some the mixture onto a hot, oiled griddle. Turn the pikelet over when the surface is looking dry. This is only a few seconds each side. Don't over cook them or they loose some of their flavour. Keep each pikelet warm whilst cooking the rest of the batter. Eat either hot from the pan with butter or honey or toast when cold. They will keep till the following day.

Cook the crumpet in a metal ring on the griddle. Allow to cook until the top looks 'set' on the top. Cook on one side only and serve toasted with butter.

Plain Breadsticks

Breadsticks can be eaten with many types of dip and soups. They are great for parties and adding cheese, herbs and seeds will vary the flavour. Breadsticks are really easy to make and taste so much better than the shop bought variety.

225g/8oz self-raising flour
1 dessert spoon sugar
1 rounded teaspoon salt
125ml/4fl oz milk
Melted butter to dip the fingers in, about 20g/1oz

Mix all the dry ingredients together. Add the milk and mix well. Knead to form a pliable dough. Roll into a rectangle about 1.5cm thick and cut into strips about 1cm wide and 12-15cm long. Dip each strip into melted butter and place on an oiled baking sheet. Bake at 200°C/Gas mark 6 for 10-15 minutes until golden brown.

Cheese Breadsticks

Add 50g/2oz strong cheddar cheese to the dry ingredients before adding the milk and continue in the same way as above.

For herb or seeded breadsticks add 1 teaspoon of dried herbs or 1 tablespoon of mixed seeds of your choice to the dry ingredients and follow the recipe as before.

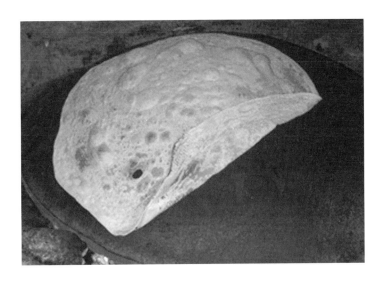

Chapter Six
Ethnic Breads

Thankfully specialist breads from all over the world can now be purchased in delicatessen shops, supermarkets and farmers markets everywhere. But have a go at making your own. They are certainly much easier than you might think.

Asia

I thought I wouldn't be able to make naan as I didn't have a tandoor oven to cook in, but my friend, Nusrut, is Kashmiri and makes them all the time in her conventional oven. This recipe is the one Nusrut makes regularly for her family.

Naan

Naan is a wonderfully soft, almost creamy tasting bread, traditionally baked in a tandoor, pressed on to the side of the oven and cooked at very high temperatures so that bubbles form in the dough. It is cooked very quickly, which keeps it soft and moist. It can be cooked in a regular oven so long as it reaches a temperature of 230°C/ Gas mark 8.

The following recipe is sufficient to serve 6 people as an accompaniment or 3 people if it is the main carbohydrate section of a meal.

225g/8oz strong white flour
½ teaspoon salt
1 sachet yeast
4 tablespoons warm milk
1 tablespoon sunflower oil
2 tablespoons plain yogurt
1 egg, beaten

Mix together the flour, salt and yeast into a bowl. Add the milk, oil, yogurt and the beaten egg. Knead for 10 minutes and leave to prove for 30 minutes. Towards the end of the proving time, heat an oiled baking sheet in a hot oven 230°C/ Gas mark 8. Divide into 3 sections and roll out into the traditional teardrop shape. Place on the hot baking sheet and put in the hottest part of your oven for 3-4 minutes.

Chapatis

Chapatis are traditionally cooked on a tava. This is a cast iron plate but they are also easily made using a large, heavy-based frying pan or a griddle and cooked lightly on both sides.

It is best to make them in batches, keeping the baked ones warm until the whole batch is cooked. These flat, unleavened rounds are made from atta flour which is made from wheat using the germ and the endosperm but not the bran. Your local Asian food store will have atta flour but many supermarkets are now starting to stock it as well. If you cannot find atta flour then wholemeal is fine.

This recipe makes approximately 8 chapatis.

225g/8oz atta/wholemeal flour
150ml-180ml/5-7 fl oz water
½ teaspoon salt

Place the flour in a bowl and add the water, combining them slowly with a wooden spoon. Knead lightly until the dough is pliable. Heat the pan over a medium heat. Divide the dough into 8 pieces and knead into a ball. Roll out on a lightly floured surface until approximately 20cm/8" in diameter. Shake off any excess flour and place in the hot frying pan. Cook for a minute or so then turn over and cook on the other side.

Poori

You can make poori in a very similar way to chapatis by just adding 2 tablespoons of sunflower oil and reducing the water by 30ml. Roll out in the same way as chapatis but cook in a little vegetable oil about 1cm deep. If the poori start to float, keep pressing them under the oil until they are light and puffy in texture. Turn the poori over for a few seconds, then place on some kitchen paper to get rid of excess oil. Keep warm if not being served straight away or they will lose their crispness.

Aloo Parathas

Potato parathas are my favourite accompaniment to Asian food. They are very tasty and I enjoy using them to pick up my food. They are a filling and satisfying bread when hungry.

400g/14oz wheatmeal flour
1 teaspoon sugar
1 teaspoon salt
230ml/8fl oz milk or water
1 egg, beaten
4 medium potatoes, boiled and mashed
2 tablespoons finely chopped, fresh coriander
30-40g/1-2oz ghee for frying

Mix the flour, sugar and salt together in a bowl. Add the beaten egg and milk and combine to form a dough. Knead until smooth. Combine the mashed potato and coriander with a little extra seasoning to taste. Divide the dough into 6 equal balls and roll out to form a flat disc. Place a tablespoon of potato mixture into the centre of the dough. Bring up the edges and moisten with a little water so that the dough sticks together. Twist the edges and flatten down. Finally turn the paratha over and roll flat.

Heat a griddle or frying pan with a generous amount of ghee. Place a paratha twist side down in the pan and cook for a few minutes. Brush the top with more ghee and turn over to cook the other side in the same way until both sides are golden brown.

Pitta Bread

Pitta bread originates in the Middle East, but is now widely popular mainly because of the way they break open and are easily filled with salads, kebabs or indeed anything you fancy. This recipe makes 8-10 pieces.

450g/1lb strong white flour
1 sachet fast action dried yeast
1 teaspoon salt
300ml/½ pint warm water

Sieve the flour and salt together into a bowl. Stir in the yeast. Make a well in the centre and pour in the water. Combine well to form a soft dough.

Knead for 10 minutes until smooth and leave to prove for 20 minutes. Break the dough into 8-10 equal pieces depending on how large you want them.

Roll out each piece into an oval shape about 4mm/1/3 inch thick. Place on a baking tray and leave to rest for 8-10 minutes. Bake in the oven at the hottest temperature (at least 230°C/Gas mark 8) for 5-8 minutes until puffed up and golden.

Chinese Pan Bread

Chinese pan bread can be served with any type of food. I enjoy them with a poached egg on top.

225g/8oz plain flour
175ml/7fl oz water
5 finely chopped spring onions
2 teaspoons sunflower oil
1 teaspoon salt

Combine the onions and oil. Sieve the flour and salt together and gradually pour in the water whilst mixing well. Knead for a few minutes until the dough is smooth.

Add the onion mixture to the dough and knead again until well combined. Divide into 4 equal pieces and knead each piece. Roll into 1cm thick rounds. Fry each round in a little oil.

Africa

Injera

Injera are a cross between a pancake and a flatbread. They are very quick to make and you can cook a lot in a short space of time. They go really well with thick stews and curries as you can scoop up the food with them as you would with a fork or spoon. They come from Ethiopia and are made from a type of flour called 'teff' that contains practically no gluten. Ordinary plain wheat flour may be substituted to make these.

300g/10oz plain flour, brown or white
450ml/12fl oz water
1/2 teaspoon salt

Mix the flour, salt and water together and beat vigorously to a smooth batter. Fry in a little oil in a hot frying pan, adding enough of the batter to coat the bottom of the pan. Slightly thicker than a crepe is about the correct thickness for injera. Cook until the upperside is dry. There is no need to turn them over as they will already be thoroughly cooked.

Coconut Bread

500g/1lb2oz plain flour
2 teaspoons baking powder
100g/4oz butter, melted
130ml/4½ fl oz milk or coconut milk
150g/5oz grated coconut
175g/6oz sugar
1 egg
½ teaspoon salt

Sift together the dry ingredients and stir in the sugar. Add the coconut and make a well in the centre of the flour. Pour in the liquid, melted butter and beaten egg. Mix together thoroughly and knead with your hands for a few minutes. Place in 2lb or two 1lb oiled loaf tins. Score the top and brush with a little water and sprinkle with sugar. Bake for 25-30 minutes at 190°C/ Gas mark 5 until golden brown. Leave to cool completely before slicing.

The Americas

Bagels

Although originally Yiddish and Eastern European in origin, it is the American market which has poularised the bagel. They are now readily available in most shops and supermarkets. These ring shaped rolls are boiled before baking. They seem a little messy to make but taste so good. My daughter loves them filled with cream cheese and smoked salmon. Very decadent! The following recipe makes 18-20 bagels.

500g/1lb strong white flour
250ml/9fl oz warm water
1 sachet fast action dried yeast
6 teaspoons caster sugar
1 teaspoon salt
2 tablespoons sunflower oil
2 eggs, beaten lightly

Mix the flour, sugar, salt and yeast together in a bowl. Make a well in the centre of the flour and pour in the water, oil and eggs, keeping a few teaspoons of egg back to glaze the bagels. Stir well and combine by hand. Knead the dough for 10 minutes until smooth. Roll into a ball, cover and leave to prove for 15 minutes. Knead again for a few minutes and shape sections of dough into rings, moistening the edges to be pinched together. Leave on a floured surface to prove for 30 minutes covered with a towel. Preheat the oven to 200°C/Gas mark 6. Meanwhile, poach the bagels in slightly salted boiling water for 15-20 seconds. Drain well and place on an oiled baking tray. Brush with the egg glaze and bake for 10-15 minutes.

Classic Cornbread

This is a basic cornbread recipe. Other ingredients can be added to vary the taste, but the main recipe remains the same and is very easy to make.

140g/5oz cornmeal (semolina)
125g/4oz plain white flour
1 teaspoon baking soda
2 eggs
115g/3½oz butter
235ml/8fl oz buttermilk
1 level teaspoon salt
1 tablespoon sugar

Melt the butter with the sugar in a large pan over a low heat. Beat in the eggs. Stir in the baking soda and buttermilk. Beat in the flour and salt to make a smooth batter. Pour the batter into a well oiled 8 inch/20cm square tin. Bake for 30–40 minutes at 180°C/Gas mark 4.

To vary this recipe:

Add 2 tablespoons of sugar, 50g/2oz of raisins or sultanas, a level teaspoon of cinnamon and a sprinkle of grated nutmeg.

Add 2 chopped jalapeno chillies or even more if you like it hot.

Add ½ teaspoon of dry mustard and 50g of grated strong cheddar or Monterey jack cheese. Sprinkle extra cheese on top when just out of the oven.

Add a small can of creamed corn or sweetcorn.

Tortillas

Tortillas are the most popular bread of Mexico and are traditionally made with maize flour. They can be eaten with most foods, especially chilli based meat and vegetable dishes. Here are two recipes, one using the traditional maize flour and the other using ordinary plain flour. The latter is lighter and good for wraps. The two recipes make 10-12 large tortillas.

Corn Tortillas

450g/1lb maize flour
175g/6oz plain white flour
1 teaspoons salt
600ml/1pint hot water

Mix the flours and salt together and slowly add the hot water. Knead for 5 minutes till smooth. Add more flour or water to get the right pliable and easy to use consistency. Divide the mixture into 10-12 pieces and roll each into a large disc that will fit into your frying pan. Heat your pan with a small amount of oil and fry each tortilla on both sides for about a minute each side. Store in the fridge wrapped in a clean, damp cloth until needed and warm in a hot frying pan when ready to serve.

Flour Tortillas

500g/1lb plain flour
1 teaspoon salt

300ml/9fl oz warm water
2 tablespoons sunflower oil

Sieve the flour and salt together into a bowl and add the water and oil. Mix well to form a ball. Knead for 4-5 minutes until the dough is no longer sticky, adding a little more flour if the mixture is too sticky. Divide the dough into 10-12 equal parts and roll each piece into a large disc as thin as manageable. Fry in a non-stick pan for a minute on both sides and pile up each tortilla on a large plate. Serve warm or cool and freeze till needed. Thaw completely before reheating in a hot frying pan.

Russia

Blini are an ancient Russian bread made from buckwheat. They can be served at breakfast or as a starter course with smoked salmon or caviar. We like to eat them with bacon and scrambled eggs.

Make as many as you can eat fresh as they don't store well. The following recipe makes 12-15 blinis and uses buckwheat flour. If you have difficulty finding it, use wholewheat flour instead.

Blini

90g/3oz buckwheat flour
60g/2oz plain flour

1 sachet fast action dried yeast
300ml/10fl oz water or ½ milk and
½ water, warmed
2 eggs, separated
½ teaspoon salt
60g/2oz melted butter
120ml/4fl oz soured cream

Sieve the flour and salt into a large bowl and stir in the yeast. Make a well in the centre of the flour and pour in the warm liquid, melted butter and egg yolks. Whisk together to make a smooth batter and add cream. Whisk this in lightly.

Leave the batter in a warm place for 45 minutes until very frothy. Whisk the egg whites until firm and fold into the batter mixture. Heat a large frying pan or griddle lightly oiled by wiping a piece of oiled kitchen paper over the cooking surface of the pan.

When hot, ladle a little of the batter into the pan to make small pancakes. Cook for a minute or so until golden, then turnthe blini over and cook for a further minute.

Keep them warm in an oven whilst cooking the rest of the batch.

Sweden

Swedish Limpa bread is a very rich, heavy bread, good to eat in the winter time when appetites

73

are hearty. It is delicious sliced and served with butter or marmalade. It keeps well in an air-tight container and is equally good toasted.

Limpa Bread

700g/1½lb rye flour
175g/6oz strong white flour
2 tablespoons dried yeast
1 teaspoon sugar
550ml/1pint warm milk
90g/3oz melted butter
1 teaspoon salt
4 tablespoons golden syrup
1 tablespoon treacle
1 teaspoon ground star anise
1 teaspoon ground fennel
Grated zest of 2 oranges

Mix the yeast with the sugar and ¼ pint of the warm milk in a large jug. Stir and leave for 10 minutes to froth.

Sieve the white flour, spices and salt together into a large bowl and stir in the rye flour. Pour the rest of the milk and the melted butter into the yeast mixture. Make a well in the centre of the flour and add the orange zest, yeast mixture, syrup and treacle. Mix thoroughly with a wooden spoon till all the flour is combined with the other ingredients.

Knead the dough for 5-10 minutes until the

mixture is smooth. Cover and leave to prove in a bowl for 45 minutes. Knock back and knead for a further 3-4 minutes. Divide the dough into 3 equal parts and form into smooth round loaves. Place on an oiled baking sheet, cover and prove for 30 minutes. Brush with water and bake at 200°C/Gas mark 6 for 30-35 minutes. Leave to cool thoroughly before slicing.

Eastern Europe

Pumpernickel is a dark rye bread that stores well and is good served with sliced meats and cheese and pickles. We like to eat it with tomatoes seasoned with salt and vinegar. This bread must be stored for 1-2 days before eating to allow the flavour to develop.

Pumpernickel

150g/5oz dark rye flour
700g/1½lb wholemeal flour
90g/3oz buckwheat flour
50g/2oz cornmeal (semolina)
2 sachets fast action dried yeast
2 teaspoons salt
1 tablespoon treacle
750ml/1¼ pints warm water

Mix the flours and salt in a large bowl and stir in the yeast. Make a well in the centre and pour in half of the water and the treacle. Mix together then add the rest of the water, mixing well with a wooden spoon. Knead the dough for 10-15 minutes until it becomes smooth and elastic. Oil two 2lb loaf tins and shape the dough into two loaf shapes. Place in the tins and leave to prove in a warm place. This will take about 45-50 minutes. The dough should rise to just above the tins. Bake at 190°C/ Gas mark 6 for 45- 50 minutes. If the dough isn't cooked after this time, cook for a further 10 minutes, checking for burning.

Italy

There are many wonderful Italian bread recipes from all the different regions throughout the country. I have included the most popular eaten in Britain and my son's own favourite, Grissini.

Grissini

900g/2lb plain white flour
1 sachet fast action dried yeast
3 teaspoons salt
1 tablespoon sugar
1 tablespoon olive oil
600ml/1pint warm water

Mix the flour, salt, sugar and yeast together in a bowl and add the water and oil. Combine well with a wooden spoon and knead for 10 minutes. Leave to prove for 30 minutes. Break off small sections of dough and roll and stretch each piece until each one measures around 30cm/12inches long. Place on an oiled baking sheet. Brush each stick with a little olive oil and sprinkle with sesame or poppy seeds if you wish.

Ciabatta

Ciabatta is one of the most popular breads in Italy and Britain alike. It needs to be left to prove for long periods of time during which the characteristic large holes are formed in the bread so it cannot be rushed. The soft textured crust is achieved by cooking the bread alongside a tin of water that evaporates whilst the bread is baking. This is a recipe I have adapted to make an easy and much quicker version.

500g/1lb strong white flour
1 sachet fast action dried yeast
2 teaspoons salt
380ml/14fl oz water

Sieve the flour and salt together into a bowl and stir in the yeast. Add the water gradually and knead in to make a smooth dough. Continue to knead for a further 10 minutes and shape into two long, flat loaves. Place on a lightly oiled baking tray. Leave to prove for 3-4 hours in a cool place, NOT A WARM PLACE! Bake for 15-20 minutes at 220°C/Gas mark 7. Place a small tray of water in the oven for 20 minutes before baking the bread, but remove before cooking.

Focaccia

Focaccia has many names in different regions of Italy, from 'Stiacciata' in Tuscany to 'Fitascetta' in Lombardy. We call it Focaccia, but whatever it is called it is a flat bread made with lots of lovely olive oil and coarse sea salt. Foccacia is an ancient bread and dates back to when baking was carried out on hot stones over an open fire. After proving, the dough is pressed flat in an oiled tray and indentations are made in the dough using the fingers. These indentations are there to catch the olive oil during the baking process. This loaf was originally made popular by the Romans and has changed very little though there are many variations cooked throughout Italy.

This loaf is traditionally cooked in an oven after the fire has been raked down, but the temperature is still too hot to cook the larger loaves without them burning. Focaccia can be eaten as an accompaniment to main dishes or soups and it makes an excellent shared starter to a meal served with olives and sun-dried tomatoes. It can be varied by topping the bread with onions, sliced olives or thinly sliced courgettes. Various cheeses can also be sprinkled on top to add flavour. The Tuscan version 'Stiacciata' is a sweetened bread that has sugar, eggs and spices added. A really tasty version is Focaccia 'al formaggio' where two thin layers of dough are rolled out and stracchino cheese spread over the layers and drizzled with olive oil and baked until the cheese melts. Some regions use polenta or buckwheat flour to make the dough. This recipe is the simplest form, but one which can be varied quite readily.

500g/1lb 2oz strong white flour
1 sachet fast action dried yeast
Approximately 180ml/6fl oz warm water
½ teaspoon salt
2 tablespoons olive oil, more for drizzling over finished bread
20g/1oz coarse sea salt

Put the flour, yeast and salt in a bowl and mix. Add the oil and water and mix thoroughly together. Knead the dough for about 10 minutes, until smooth and elastic. Leave to prove in a warm place for 40 minutes. Heat the oven to 225°C/ Gas mark 7. After proving, press the dough out onto an oiled baking tray until it measures about 2cm in thickness. Press the fingertips into the dough to make indentations and drizzle with olive oil. Sprinkle with sea salt and bake for about 25 minutes until golden brown, then drizzle more oil over the hot bread. Allow to cool and cut into rectangles. The flavour is wonderful!

France

The French love their fresh bread and, despite their huge supermarkets, the local traditional boulangerie still continues to provide much of the nation's daily fresh bread. When we were on holiday in a little Northern French hamlet the local baker came round selling his fresh baguettes and rolls every morning. It is difficult to achieve the same texture and taste of real French bread, but the following recipes are still delicious and reminiscent of the freshest bread you would find in France.

French Stick or Baguette

450g/1lb strong white flour
1 sachet fast action dried yeast
1 teaspoon salt
300ml/½ pint warm water
Egg to glaze

Sieve the flour and salt together into a bowl and stir in the yeast. Mix in the warm water and knead for 10 minutes. Leave to prove in a warm place for 20 minutes. Knock back and knead for a few more minutes. Divide into 3 equal sections and shape into a 30cm/12 inch long roll. Place on an oiled baking sheet and leave to prove for 30 minutes. Brush with beaten egg to glaze. Bake for 15-20 minutes at 220°C/Gas mark 7.

Brioche

Brioche is my favourite breakfast roll when in France and is delicious with French preserves. They keep well for a few days in an air-tight tin and are best warmed if more than a day old. The following recipe makes 15-20 brioches.

450g/1lb strong white flour
1 sachet fast action dried yeast
2 level teaspoons salt
225g/8oz melted butter
90ml/3fl oz warm milk
4 eggs, beaten
1 tablespoon golden caster sugar

Sieve the flour and salt together into a bowl and stir in the yeast. Add the milk, butter and beaten eggs (leaving a little to glaze the brioches with before baking) and mix thoroughly with a wooden spoon. Knead for 10 minutes until smooth and pliable. Break off small amounts of dough and roll into oval shapes, placing them on an oiled baking sheet. Repeat until all the dough is used. Four larger brioches may be made if preferred. Leave to prove for 30 minutes, then brush with the remaining egg. Bake for 10-15 minutes for the small brioches or 15-20 minutes for the larger ones at 220°C/Gas mark 7.

Croissants

When most people are asked what a traditional French breakfast consists of they would probably say croissants and coffee. But we enjoy them at teatime with preserves as well as at breakfast. They are complicated to make and take up the best part of an afternoon, but they are well worth the effort. They also freeze well and cook quickly.

1kg/2lb 2oz strong white flour

450g/1lb unsalted butter, cut into cubes
½ teaspoon salt
280ml/½ pint water
280ml/½ pint milk
2 sachets fast action dried yeast

Sieve the flour and salt together into a bowl and stir in the yeast. Add the butter and mix into the flour using a palette knife. Add the milk and water and knead lightly to form a dough. Roll out on a lightly floured surface to form a large rectangle. Turn the top third down and seal and turn the bottom third up and seal the edges. Chill for 30 minutes. Repeat the last step 3 more times, turning the dough by 90° each time. Finally, roll out the dough into a large rectangle and cut in half. Cut each rectangle into 12 small triangles. Roll up each triangle from the widest part and form a crescent shape. Place each of them on an oiled baking sheet. The croissants may be frozen at this stage or glazed with beaten egg and baked for 15-20 minutes at 200°C/Gas mark 6.
Defrost completely before glazing and baking.

The above is only a small selection of the variety of breads from all over the world. I am sure I have missed out many others but the list will give you a broad understanding of cooking with yeast and will hopefully prompt you to go on to further develop your skills in the craft of bread making

Chapter Seven
Sweetened Breads

When I first began cooking with yeast I slipped into the common assumption that it is only used for making loaves and rolls. There are, however, so many wonderful recipes for both bread and bread related products that I would never be able to fit them into this book. This section focuses on sweetened doughs that make delicious teabreads and desserts. They are easy to make and come in all shapes and sizes. Most recipes keep better than other unsweetened doughs as they contain more fat and, of course, sugar, both of which act as a preservative. The first section covers individual buns or teacakes.

Twin Rose Teacakes

Teacakes originate from both Yorkshire and Lancashire – hence the name. They have always been a popular tea break treat and I remember coming home from school on a wintery days to a mug of cocoa and a hot, toasted teacake.

Teacakes are thought to be descendants of a medieval 'hand-bread' or 'manchet.' these were small, hand-shaped loaves made with the finest flour of the time and cooked without a tin. They can be made without dried fruit for those who dislike it, but personally I love the fruited version. Spices such as cinnamon and nutmeg may be included in the recipe, but I prefer to save this for hot cross buns.

450g/1lb strong white flour
1 sachet fast action dried yeast
300ml warm milk
50g/2oz currants (rinsed and dried)
50g/2oz sultanas (rinsed and dried)
40g/1.5oz softened butter
50g/2oz sugar
1 level teaspoon salt

Mix the flour and salt together in a large mixing bowl and add the yeast. Rub in the butter and add the sugar. Make a well in the centre of the flour and add the milk, stirring in well. Then knead the dough till smooth. Next knead in the dried fruit and continue to knead for a further 5 minutes.

Divide the dough into 10-12 small balls, knead into ball shapes and roll into 9cm discs. Place on an oiled baking tray and leave to prove for 20-30 minutes. Bake in a hot oven at 225°C/gas mark 8 for 10 minutes. Cool and serve with butter and/or some homemade preserve or honey.

Farthing Buns

In the later years of Queen Victoria's reign Farthing buns, as the name suggests, cost a farthing each, which was quite expensive at the time, but they are very rich and buttery and a real treat. This recipe makes between 20 and 25 buns.

450g/1lb strong white flour
1 sachet fast action dried yeast
220ml/8fl oz warm milk or milk and water mixed
½ teaspoon salt
100g/4oz unrefined caster sugar
50g/2oz butter, gently melted, but not hot
125g/4oz mixed dried fruit
1 large egg, beaten
Unrefined granulated sugar for sprinkling
Melted butter for brushing

Sieve the flour and salt together and stir in the yeast and sugar. Add the liquid, butter and beaten egg (saving a little to glaze the buns with). Mix thoroughly with a wooden spoon.
Add the dried fruit gradually whilst kneading it

in with your hands. Keep kneading the dough for 8 minutes, then leave to prove for 20 minutes. Roll out the dough to a rectangle about 5mm/¼ inch thick and brush with melted butter over the top two thirds of the dough. Fold the unbuttered third up over the centre section and the remaining section over the others. Leave to rest for 10 minutes.

Roll out the dough in the same way, but brush the whole surface with butter and sprinkle with sugar. Then cut the dough into rectangles approximately 8cm/3 inches by 3cm/1¼ inches and place them on an oiled baking sheet. Leave to prove in a warm place for 20-30 minutes. Bake for 10-12 minutes at 220°C/Gas mark 7.

Chelsea Buns

My first encounter with making Chelsea buns was not a happy one. I was at school and studying for my O' level examinations. My cookery lesson that morning was being taught by a student teacher and I was eagerly looking forward to it as we were to make Chelsea buns. Already confident about making bread I thought that this lesson would be enjoyable but during the process of rolling out the dough and sprinkling the work surface with what I thought was flour in a shaker, something very strange started to happen to my dough. It began running off the table, like a grey, yeasty liquid. The poor student was flabbergasted, called me a fool and told me to clear up the mess. She hadn't a clue what had happened and sent for my regular cookery teacher.

Miss Christie looked at me and smiled, 'There is icing sugar in your shaker, not flour. You have over-fed your yeast. Diana, you will have to start again.' I did, and they turned out fine. I never did find out whether the student ever became a fully fledged teacher!

250g/8oz strong white flour
1 teaspoon dried yeast
½ teaspoon sugar, for the yeast
90ml/3fl oz warm milk
25g/1oz melted butter
½ teaspoon salt
1 egg, beaten
75g/3oz raisins
1 tablespoon candied peel
25g/1oz melted butter for brushing over dough
50g/2oz demerera sugar
Honey for glazing

Mix the dried yeast with the sugar and warm milk and leave to froth up for 10 minutes. Meanwhile, sieve the flour and salt into a bowl and add the yeast mixture, butter and beaten egg. Mix together and knead until smooth for about 10 minutes. Cover the dough and leave in a warm place to prove for about 40 minutes.
Roll out the dough into a rectangle measuring about 32cm by 22cm/13 inches by 9 inches. Brush with melted butter and sprinkle with sugar, dried fruit and peel. Starting with the longest edge, roll

up the dough into a long sausage shape and cut out 9 slices. Place each slice cut side up on an oiled baking sheet. Keep them close together as they should meet when they are cooking.

Leave to prove for 30 minutes and then bake for 20-25 minutes at 220°C/Gas mark 7 till golden brown.

Brush the hot buns with honey to glaze.

Bath Buns

Bath buns can be made with or without fruit, depending on your preference. If you want to omit the fruit from the following recipe just exclude it but do add the grated lemon zest as this lifts the flavour of the buns. They are very easy to make and this will provide about 15 buns.

275g/10oz strong white flour
25g/1oz unrefined caster sugar
150ml/¼ pint warm milk
75g/3oz melted butter
½ sachet fast action dried yeast
1 egg, beaten
Zest of 1 lemon
100g/4oz sultanas
25g/1oz candied peel
50g/2oz crushed brown lump sugar or sugar cubes

Sieve the flour and salt into a bowl and stir in the sugar and yeast. Pour in the warm milk, butter and egg. Mix together well with a wooden spoon. Knead in the fruit, peel, lemon zest and crushed sugar lumps and continue to knead for 10 minutes. Divide the dough into 15 equal pieces, place on an oiled baking tray and leave to prove for 30-35 minutes.

Brush with milk and sprinkle each bun with a little more crushed sugar. Bake for 10 minutes at 220°C/ Gas mark 7.

Honey and Raisin Buns

These soft buns owe their light-texture to their yogurt and egg white content. They don't contain yeast so are very quick to make. This recipe makes about 12 buns.

300g/10oz plain flour
2 teaspoons baking powder
½ teaspoon salt
50g raisins
2 tablespoons honey
300ml/10fl oz plain, runny yogurt
2 whisked egg whites

Sieve the flour, salt and baking powder together into a bowl. Stir in the yogurt, honey and raisins and fold in the egg whites. Put a heaped tablespoon of the mixture into each compartment of a non-stick muffin tin and bake for 15-20 minutes at 220°C/Gas mark 7.

Lemon Curd Buns

When I serve these buns to friends and family I don't tell them about the hidden centre which makes it a delicious surprise. These lemon curd buns bring a smile to everyone who eats them.

400g/14oz strong white flour
1 sachet fast action dried yeast
½ level teaspoon salt
75g/3oz sugar
1 egg, beaten
220ml/8oz warm water
75g/2oz melted butter
Lemon curd for filling
Melted butter for brushing the dough
Beaten egg to glaze
Unrefined caster sugar to sprinkle on buns

Sieve most of the flour and salt together and stir in the sugar and yeast. Pour in the water and butter and mix thoroughly. Add the beaten egg and the rest of the flour and knead well for 10 minutes to make a smooth dough. Leave to prove for 20 minutes. Break off small amounts of dough and roll them into small discs, about 3mm thick. Brush with butter and place a teaspoon of lemon curd in the centre of the disc. Fold in half and seal the edges well. Brush once more with butter and fold and seal again. Place on an oiled baking sheet and leave to prove for 20 minutes. Brush with beaten egg and sprinkle with sugar. Bake for 10-12 minutes at 220°C/Gas mark 7.

Sally Lunn Loaf

The next recipe can be made into 3 medium sized loaves as described or individual rolls. This recipe will make about 8 individual rolls. The Sally Lunn loaf is named after the lady who first made it. Sally Lunn was a celebrated pastry cook who lived in Bath in the 1780s and owned a shop in Lilliput Alley.

Sally Lunn sold her wares to the rich and fashionable people of the time who came to sample the local waters. The cakes and breads were sold in the Pump Room and eaten alongside the drinking of the water. Her shop is still there to visit.

This loaf is best eaten warm with generous amounts of butter, but be careful when slicing. Use a very sharp knife as it can be a bit tricky.

280g/$\frac{1}{2}$lb strong white flour
1 sachet fast action dried yeast
150ml/5fl oz warm water
40g/1$\frac{1}{2}$ oz.sugar
50g/2 oz softened butter
1 large egg, beaten
Finely grated rind of 1 lemon
$\frac{1}{2}$ teaspoon salt

Sift the flour into a bowl and stir in the salt. Add the yeast and mix in thoroughly. Make a well in centre of the flour and add the sugar, egg and

lemon rind. Add the water and mix in vigorously.
Next knead in the butter and continue to knead
the dough till smooth for approximately 5
minutes.
Divide the dough into 3 equal parts and knead
each section, shaping each one into a round and
place them on an oiled baking tray, leaving them
to prove in a warm place for about 30 minutes.
Brush with beaten egg and bake in a hot oven at
225°C/Gas mark 8 for 15 minutes.

Selkirk Bannocks

The next recipe is for Scottish Selkirk bannocks.
The bannock is a flat loaf the size of a large tea
plate. It is this shape because it was traditionally
cooked on a flat, griddle pan. They contain a lot
of fruit so they are very wholesome. This recipe
makes 3 good sized loaves.

450g/1lb strong white flour
1 sachet fast action dried yeast
1 level teaspoon salt
60g/2oz sugar
80g/3oz melted butter
450g/1lb sultanas or a mixture of raisins,
currants and sultanas
300ml/½ pint warm milk
Honey to glaze

Sieve the flour and salt together into a bowl
and stir in the yeast and sugar. Make a well in
the centre and add the milk and butter. Mix

thoroughly until all the ingredients are combined and knead in the fruit and continue to knead for a further 10 minutes.

Shape the dough into 3 rounds and flatten well with the hands. Place on an oiled baking sheet and leave to prove for 30-40 minutes. Flatten the bannocks a little with your hands again if they have puffed up too much.

Bake for 20 minutes at 220°C/Gas mark 7.

Tea Loaves

Tea loaves are wonderfully versatile and just the thing to serve with hot drinks when people visit or just when you are peckish. Some recipes produce a bread like finish because they contain yeast and others are more cake like in texture as the raising agent used is baking powder. This means that there is a great variety of tea loaf recipes, many of them very easy to make.

Marmalade Tea Loaf

My first recipe is for a very simple old-fashioned marmalade tea loaf. This was a favourite with my uncle who always asked my Mum to bake one when he came to visit. The marmalade gives the loaf a really tangy flavour and it has the added benefit of keeping it moist, which some tea loaves lack. Just because we are going to drink tea with them it doesn't mean they should be dry. The other benefit of this recipe is that you don't need butter and is delicious eaten without.

Marmalade Tea Loaf

200g/8oz self-raising flour
1 teaspoon cinnamon
100g/4oz butter, cut into small pieces
60g/2½ oz Muscovado sugar
1 egg
3 tablespoons marmalade
3 tablespoons milk
A little extra marmalade for the top

Sift the flour and cinnamon into a bowl. Add the butter and rub in with the fingertips. When the mixture looks like breadcrumbs, stir in the sugar. Beat the egg and mix the milk and marmalade together. Add the milk mixture and the beaten egg. Beat these in well with a wooden spoon.

Transfer the mixture to a greased 1lb loaf tin and cook for 55-65 minutes in an oven heated to 160°C/Gas mark 3.

When the cooking time is complete, cool slightly then brush the top of the cake with a little warmed marmalade. This can be done by using a hot spoon to hold the marmalade whilst brushing the top of the cake.

If you have problems with your Muscovado sugar being lumpy as I did, place it in a bowl covered with a damp tea cloth for an hour and the sugar will regain its correct texture. This happens because the sugar dries up in the packet and needs a little re-moistening.

Pecan Tea Loaf

My next recipe is for Pecan bread (or walnuts, whichever you prefer). It is also very easy if you use the fast action dried yeast and is very similar to making bread. The dough must be kneaded and, as it contains dried fruit and nuts, some people prefer to add these whilst they knead the dough, but I find it easier to put the fruit and nuts in the mixture before adding the liquid. Either way the finished loaf is the same.

450g/1lb strong white flour
1 teaspoon salt
1 sachet fast action dried yeast
40g/1½ oz unrefined caster sugar
50g/2oz butter
280ml/10fl oz milk
50g/2oz pecans
220g/9oz dried fruit (a mixture of sultanas, raisins and chopped apricots or your favourite mixture)

Put the butter and milk in a pan over a very low heat till the butter has melted. Meanwhile, sieve the flour and salt into a large mixing bowl. Add the dried yeast and stir. Mix in the sugar and dried fruits and nuts. Make a well in the centre of the flour mixture and pour in the butter and milk. Stir thoroughly with a wooden spoon. Knead the dough for 10 minutes. Place in a greased tin and leave to prove in a warm place for 35-40 mins. Bake at 225°C/Gas mark 7 for 15-20 mins.

Bara Brith

I have found and tried many recipes for Bara Brith, the Welsh fruited tea loaf, (the name means 'speckled bread'). Some contain yeast and others use self-raising flour. If yeast is used, the Bara Brith will be more like bread and without yeast the finished product is more like eating cake. Have a go at both and see which you prefer.

The first recipe is very easy and makes for a really fruity finish to the loaf. The second is a little more work and uses less fruit.

Bara Brith No.1

400g/1lb self-raising flour
350g/10oz mixed raisins, currants and sultanas
candied peel (if you wish)
275ml/½ pint of cold tea
2 tablespoons honey
1 egg, beaten
80g/3oz soft brown sugar
1 teaspoon mixed spice

Soak the fruit in the tea overnight. Sift the flour and spice into a large mixing bowl and stir in the sugar. Add the fruit and tea mixture, the egg and honey and stir thoroughly. Pour the mixture into a buttered 2lb loaf tin and cook for 1½-1¾ hours at 170°C/Gas mark 3.

Steps to Making a Simple Loaf

1. Mix your flour and salt together

2. Sieve together to mix well

3. Add the fast acting yeast

4. Make a well

5. Gradually add the water

6. Add a table-spoon of oil

7. Mix well

8. Is your mixture too wet?

9. Then add a little more flour

10. The final dough isn't sticky

How to Knead

1. Stretch the dough forwards

2. Pull the stretched dough over to the bottom

3. Push the dough down with the fists

4. Turn the dough by 90 ° and repeat

5.When you get into a rhythm use your fist to pull against

6. The dough is ready to shape

Making Butter

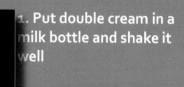

1. Put double cream in a milk bottle and shake it well

2. Cut open the bottle and keep the buttermilk for baking

3. Wash the rest of the buttermilk away with cold water

4. shape your butter and store

5. Ready when you are

Milly's All Bran Loaf

Marmalade Tea Loaf

Slices of Sally Lunn

Bara Brith No. 2

300g/10oz strong white flour
220g/9oz mixed dried fruit
25g/1oz melted butter
1 egg, beaten
170ml/6fl oz warm water
30g/1½ oz unrefined caster sugar
1 sachet fast action dried yeast
1 level teaspoon salt
½ level teaspoon mixed spice

Sift the flour, spice and salt together into a large mixing bowl. Stir in the yeast and sugar. Make a well in the flour and add the water, melted butter and beaten egg, stirring thoroughly. Knead the dough for 10 minutes, adding a little more flour if it gets too sticky. Place the dough in a 2lb loaf tin and leave it to prove for 30-40minutes. After proving, bake for 10 minutes at 200°C/ Gas mark 6, then turn the oven down to 180°C/ Gas mark 4 and cook for a further 30 minutes. When cooked, brush the top of the loaf with some clear honey.

Millie's Easy All Bran Loaf

My mum said that you only need to remember two things with regard to her famous All Bran Loaf. One is to soak the fruit and All Bran the night before and the other is that all the ingredients (except the milk) are the same amounts, ie. one cup of each ingredient. So how easy is that?

Millie's All Bran Tea Loaf

1 cup All Bran
1 cup sultanas and raisins
1 cup tea
1 cup unrefined sugar
1 cup self-raising flour
5 tablespoons milk

Mix the All Bran, fruit and tea and leave overnight. Stir in the flour, milk and sugar and combine well. Pour into a buttered 1lb loaf tin and cook for 1 hour at 185°C/Gas mark 5. If it looks as though the top of the loaf is cooking too quickly turn the heat down to 170°C/Gas mark 4 and cover the top with foil. Sometimes, for a change, Mum would make it with chopped dates and walnuts in place of the dried fruit stated in this recipe. So long as it is just 1 cup you could use any dried fruits or a combination of fruit and nuts. They were all delicious sliced with a good slathering of butter. Leave to mature for 24 hours before eating if you can. My mum had to hide it from us till it was ready to eat.

Farmhouse Malt Loaf

This recipe is for a true malt loaf. We often have this as dessert with a hot drink after a meal. It is also good served with a strong flavoured cheese like Stilton or farmhouse cheddar. This malt loaf must also be left for 2-3 days to allow the flavours to develop and for it to moisten and acquire that traditional sticky texture. It is also easy to overcook it as the colour is dark to begin with and it takes quite a long time to cook. Always check the loaf after about 50 minutes by testing how firm the mixture is. If it has stopped being too springy then it is probably cooked. It will depend on your oven and, as with all recipes, you know your oven. The temperatures and cooking times are only a guide.

225g/½lb self-raising flour
225g/½lb sultanas
50g/2 oz Muscovado sugar
170g/6fl oz malt extract
1 tablespoon black treacle
2 eggs
150ml/5fl oz tea

Sift the flour into a bowl and stir in the fruit. Heat the malt, treacle and sugar gently in a pan, then pour over the flour and stir. Add the beaten eggs and tea. Beat the mixture well till smooth and completely combined. Pour into 2 buttered 1lb loaf tins and bake for 1 hour at 150°C/Gas mark 2.

If you have difficulty finding malt extract, try your local health food store or home brew shop as they usually sell it. It also comes in handy when you are making your own beer! Do remember that malt for cooking attracts no VAT but for brewing purposes it does. How confusing!

Dessert Breads

My next few recipes all make a delicious after-lunch dessert instead of cake.

Apple Bread

For the dough:
1kg/2lb 2oz strong white flour
2 sachets fast action dried yeast
250ml/8fl oz warmed milk
220g/8oz unrefined caster sugar
1 teaspoon salt
200g/6oz melted butter
3 eggs
For the topping:
2 sliced dessert apples or 1 large Bramley
2 tablespoons Demerera sugar
1 level teaspoon cinnamon
A little grated nutmeg
Melted butter for brushing

For the dough, sieve the flour and salt and stir in the sugar and yeast. Make a well in the centre of the flour and pour in the milk, eggs and melted butter. Stir all the ingredients together and combine and knead the dough by hand for 8-10 minutes until smooth. Leave to prove for 20 minutes. Oil a 30cm by 20cm non-stick roasting tin. Roll out the dough to fit the tin. Brush the dough with butter and place the apple slices in neat rows up and down the dough, over-lapping them. Leave to prove for 15 minutes.

Sprinkle the sugar and spices over the top and bake at 200°C/Gas mark 6 for 25 –35 minutes until golden brown.

Chocolate Bread

For those who love chocolate, try this chocolate bread. I was sceptical at first about this one, but once I had tasted it I was hooked. The smell when cooking is amazing and even had my neighbour knocking on the door asking me what I was baking.

350g/12oz strong white flour
3 tablespoons cocoa powder
50g soft brown sugar
1 sachet fast action dried yeast
1 teaspoon salt
30g/1^1/$_2$ oz melted butter
250ml/9fl oz warm milk
100g/4oz dark chocolate, broken into pieces

Sieve the flour, cocoa and salt into a bowl and stir in the sugar and yeast. Add the milk and melted butter and mix together well. Knead for 10 minutes. Flatten the dough, press in some of the chocolate and knead again for a few seconds. Repeat this until all the chocolate has finally been incorporated. Place in a 1lb oiled loaf tin and leave to prove for 30-40 minutes. Bake at 220°C/Ga mark 7 for 20-30 minutes. This is tricky as you cannot tell when it is cooked as it is brown already, so touch the surface of the crust. It should feel firm. Also, take it out of the tin using an oven glove and test the base for the thudding sound which indicates fully cooked. See the 'Techniques' chapter for a full description of this process.

Doughnuts

Doughnuts are very popular and, so long as you have a good deep fat frying pan, they are quite easy to make. Plain white flour can be used in this recipe as it gives the doughnuts a more cake like texture.

1lb plain white flour
1 sachet fast action dried yeast
100g/3^1/2 oz caster sugar
1 egg, beaten
50g/2oz melted butter
1 level teaspoon salt
230ml/8fl oz warm milk
Sugar for sprinkling over the doughnuts

Sieve the flour and salt together into a bowl and stir in the sugar and yeast. Add the milk, egg and butter and stir well. Use your hands to combine and form a soft dough. Knead for about 5 minutes till the dough is smooth and not sticky. I don't bother making rings. I simply roll the dough into small balls. It is easier when proving and they taste equally good. Leave the dough balls to prove for 20 minutes on a lightly oiled baking sheet. Meanwhile, heat your frying pan or deep fat fryer until very hot and try a small piece of dough to test the heat. It should begin frying immediately, otherwise your doughnuts will be very greasy and inedible. Fry the doughnuts in batches of 4-5, taking great care to drain the oil away and placing them on kitchen paper before finally rolling them in sugar. Frying takes 5-7 minutes depending on the size of doughnut.

Savarin

A savarin is very similar to a rum baba but is larger and is often laden with fruit. They make an excellent dessert and are an unusual finale to a dinner party served with any kind of cream or ice cream. They are traditionally laced with rum, but this is optional. Brandy or fruit liqueurs or simply fruit juices are an alternative. You will need a savarin or a ring mould to cook the dessert in.

Fruit Savarin

For the dough:
100g/4oz strong white flour
1/2 sachet fast action dried yeast
1/2 level teaspoon salt
2 tablespoons caster sugar
50ml/3fl oz warm milk
2 eggs, beaten
50g/2oz melted butter
For the syrup:
220g/7oz caster sugar
Either 150ml/5fl oz water or fruit juice

103

8 tablespoons dark rum
For the fruit topping:
20 black grapes, halved and seeded
20 green grapes, halved and seeded
2 kiwi fruits, peeled and sliced
1 orange, peeled and segmented
10 strawberries, hulled and halved

Sieve the flour and salt into a bowl and stir in the yeast and sugar. Add the eggs, milk and butter and mix vigorously. You don't knead with your hands for this recipe but you must beat the mixture for a few minutes until the dough becomes elastic and smooth. Place the dough in the oiled mould and leave to prove until it reaches the top of the tin. Bake at 200°C/Gas mark 6 for 25-30 minutes until golden brown.

To make the syrup put the juice/water and sugar in a pan and bring to the boil. Turn down the heat and simmer gently until the sugar has dissolved. Add the rum and leave to cool slightly. Turn the savarin out on to a cooling rack and prick all over with a skewer. Drizzle the syrup over the savarin, leaving 3-4 tablespoons for the fruit and leave to cool completely.

Place the savarin onto a serving plate and arrange the fruit in the centre. Finish by drizzling the remaining syrup over the fruit, plus a little more rum if you wish. You may use any of your favourite fruit in any combination so long as it fills the centre of the savarin generously.

Chapter Eight
Celebration Breads

Special bread recipes have often been saved for special occasions and celebrations all over the world. They usually have a deeply religious meaning or are steeped in family tradition.

I was always impressed as a child with the huge wheatsheaf loaf that was the traditional centrepiece at our Harvest Festival in Church. This chapter includes some of my own personal favourites that I have encountered over the years and now take great pleasure in making as gifts for both family and friends.

Northern Christmas Loaf

This recipe was one my Grandma made during the First World War in place of a Christmas cake. It looks a little like a Christmas cake due to the addition of black treacle to the dough. It was a complicated dough to make because of all the additions, so I have simplified it.

300g/10oz strong white flour
1 sachet fast action dried yeast
100ml/3fl oz warm milk
1 level teaspoon salt
125g/4oz melted butter
125g/4oz soft brown sugar
1 tablespoon black treacle
1 egg, beaten
1 level teaspoon each of cinnamon, mixed spice and nutmeg
220g/7oz currants
125g/4oz sultanas
125g/4oz raisins
30g/1oz mixed candied peel
Honey for glazing

Sieve the flour, salt and spices together into a bowl. Stir in the sugar and yeast. Add the milk, egg, treacle and butter and mix well. Knead the dough and add the dried fruit gradually, kneading until all the fruit is incorporated. Continue to knead until the dough is smooth. If the dough looks dry, add a little warm water whilst kneading or if it is too wet add a little extra flour. Shape the dough to fit into a 2lb loaf tin that has been oiled lightly. Leave to prove for 30-40 minutes. Bake for 40-50 minutes at 200°C/Gas mark 6. After baking, glaze the top of the loaf with lots of honey.

Stollen

Stollen is an Austrian bread eaten at Christmas time and is one of my favourites due to the marzipan which runs down the centre of the loaf. It is very rich and filling and delicious with what we call Christmas coffee; simply a mug of fresh coffee with splash of brandy. This loaf keeps well as the surface of the crust is sealed with butter and sugar after cooking.

380g/12oz strong white flour
2 tablespoons dried yeast mixed with 3 tablespoons warm milk and 1 teaspoon sugar
5 tablespoons caster sugar
280g/9oz melted butter
1/2 teaspoon salt
250ml/8fl oz warm milk
180g/6oz raisins
90g/3oz sultanas
90g/3oz candied peel
90g/3oz chopped glace cherries
50g/2oz chopped almonds
1 level teaspoon cinnamon
A little grated nutmeg
250g/8oz pack marzipan
Icing sugar for dusting

Pour the yeast mixture into a warm bowl and add the rest of the milk. Leave for 10 minutes till frothy. Meanwhile, sieve the flour, salt and spices together into a separate bowl and stir in the sugar. Pour the melted butter into the fermenting mixture and stir. Gradually add the spicy flour to the yeast mixture and knead to form a smooth dough. A few minutes should be sufficient. Leave to prove for 35-45 minutes. Knead in the fruit and nuts until everything is incorporated. Divide the mixture into 2 equal parts and roll out each section or flatten with fingers into a rough rectangle. Divide the marzipan into 2 equal parts and roll it into a sausage shape to fit down the centre of the stollen dough. Moisten the edges and roll the dough round the marzipan. Flatten the loaf and place it on an oiled baking sheet. Leave to prove for 20-25 minutes. Bake for 20-30 minutes at 200°C/Gas mark 6. Brush the baked loaves with the melted butter and dust heavily with icing sugar.

Pandolce

Pandolce, or sweet bread, is a loaf that hails from Genoa in Italy and is similar to the Panettone made in Milan. It is, however, a smaller loaf, though it still takes a long time to prepare and bake. They are normally made using two sets of dough and then combining the two after the first dough has been allowed to prove for 10-12 hours. Another dough is also prepared using all the fruit and flavourings in the recipe. Then the two doughs are combined, kneaded together and then left for a further 10-12 hours to prove before baking. The bakers spend a whole day preparing this bread and it is a very special and unique taste. I made the first dough late one evening and finished the rest the next day. By 10 o'clock that evening the Pandolce was cooked but I was too tired to eat any. Not true! It was amazing and kept for 2-3 days in an air tight container.

For the first dough

300g/10oz strong white flour
1/2 tablespoon dried yeast mixed with a teaspoon sugar and 2 tablespoons of the warm liquid, left to ferment for 10 minutes till frothy
230ml/7fl oz warm milk

Sieve the flour into a bowl and add the yeast mixture and the milk. Knead the dough until smooth. It should be very moist but easy to handle. Leave to prove for 10-12 hours. If after 10 hours the dough is leaning go onto the next stage. Don't leave it any longer.

For the second dough

650g/1lb 7oz strong white flour
200g/7oz unrefined caster sugar
150g/5oz very soft butter
2 tablespoons freshly squeezed orange juice and the zest of 1 orange

125ml/4fl oz Moscato or other dessert wine
60g/2oz candied peel
60g/2oz sultanas
1 level teaspoon fennel seeds

Sieve the flour into a bowl and stir in the sugar. Add all the other ingredients and combine thoroughly by hand. Knead well for a few minutes before combining with the first dough and knead for 5 minutes until smooth. Place in an oiled 25cm/10 inch cake tin. Use one that has sides deep enough to contain the majority of the dough as it rises. Leave for at least a further 10 hours and for up to 12 hours if it needs the extra time. Bake for 45-55 minutes at 200°C/Gas mark 6 until the bread is a deep golden colour. Allow to cool in the tin for 20 minutes before removing and placing on a cooling rack.

This is best eaten within 2 days to eat it at its best. We enjoy it with a glass of the dessert wine in the recipe. If by any chance the loaf isn't finished within 2 days it is delicious sliced, fried in a little butter and eaten with some real vanilla ice cream.

Greek Easter Loaf

There are lots of special foods made specifically for Easter celebrations. This is a recipe for a Greek Easter loaf made from a plaited dough formed into a ring with two or three painted hard boiled eggs placed in the centre. It makes an excellent centrepiece for an Easter Sunday table.

1kg/2lb 2oz strong white flour
1 sachet fast action dried yeast
380/13fl oz warm milk
150g/5oz melted butter
Grated zest of 2 lemons
4 eggs, beaten
1 teaspoon salt
50g chopped almonds
Halved (or slivers of) almonds for the top
decoration

Sieve the flour and salt together and stir in the sugar, chopped almonds and lemon zest. Add the milk, eggs and butter and combine with a wooden spoon. Mix all the ingredients together well by hand and knead for 10 minutes.

Divide the dough into three equal parts This is important as the loaf will look odd with uneven plaits. Weigh each section if necessary.

Roll each section into a sausage shape that measures about 60cm/24 inches long, plait the three sections and form into a ring. Moisten the edges if you are having trouble sticking all the ends together.

Place on an oiled baking sheet and place the hard-boiled eggs in the centre. Leave to prove for 25-30 minutes. The dough will surround the eggs and make a 'nest.'

Bake for 25-30 minutes at 190°C/Gas mark 5. After cooking paint the eggs with food colouring.

Kulich

This is a Russian Easter cake made from cream cheese and dried fruit and, not surprisingly, it uses vodka to soak the saffron, but if you prefer you can use lukewarm water instead. It is a very sweet bread and you may use less sugar if it is too sweet.

450g/1lb strong white flour
1 sachet fast action dried yeast
6 tablespoons warm water
4 strands saffron, soaked in 2 tablespoons vodka or water
$1/2$ teaspoon salt
300g/10oz caster sugar
250g/9oz raisins
100g/4oz chopped almonds
60g/20oz candied peel
1 teaspoon vanilla extract
220g/8oz melted butter
Glace icing made with 100g/4oz icing sugar and enough water to make a thick but spreadable iced topping
5-6 glace cherries

Sieve the flour and salt together and stir in the sugar and yeast. Add the water, vanilla, butter and saffron liquor and mix with a wooden spoon.Knead in the nuts and fruit and continue to knead for a further 10 minutes. Shape into a long, rounded loaf, place on an oiled baking sheet and leave to prove for 20-25 minutes. Due to the high sugar content the yeast will work very quickly so it doesn't need a long proving time. Bake for 25-30 minutes at 200°C/Gas mark 6 and, when cool, coat the top with the glace icing and decorate with glace cherries.

Casatiello

This wonderful savoury bread is a traditional part of the Easter celebrations in Naples. It uses three different types of cheese and dried Neapolitan sausage. To give the best and most authentic flavour the recipe should contain lard instead of butter and, like the Greek Easter loaf, has hard-boiled eggs nestling in the centre. This recipe makes six large rolls.

500g/1lb 1oz strong white flour
1 tablespoon dried yeast mixed with 1 teaspoon sugar and 3 tablespoons warm water
200g/7oz melted lard
1 teaspoon salt
75g/3oz each of Parmesan, Pecorino and Provolone cheeses
100g/4oz chopped Italian sausage
Ground black pepper
6 hard boiled eggs

Sieve the flour and salt into a bowl and add the yeast mixture, lard and warm water. Mix to form a dough and knead for 10 minutes. Leave to prove for 50-55 minutes or until the dough has doubled in size. Knock back the dough and flatten with the hands into a deep rectangle and sprinkle a third of the mixed cheeses and a third of the sausage onto the dough. Sprinkle with ground black pepper and fold a third up over a third of the dough and the final third over the top of the others. Repeat this step twice more without the knocking back stage.

Divide the mixture into 6 equal sections and roll into rounds. Place on an oiled baking sheet and allow to prove for 45- 50 minutes.

Press an egg into the centre of each roll, gently pushing it in about half way down into the dough. Bake for 30-40 minutes at 200°C/Gas mark 6. The bread will keep for 2-3 days if stored in an airtight container.

Hot Cross Buns

These buns are baked to remember Christ's crucifixion and have been baked on Good Friday for centuries. This recipe is easy to make and they are delicious toasted the next day. This makes about 12 buns.

450g/1lb strong white flour
1 sachet fast action dried yeast
1 level teaspoon salt
220ml/8fl oz warm milk
100g/4oz currants
50g/2oz sultanas
25g/1oz candied peel
2 teaspoons mixed spice
Zest of 1 lemon

80g/3oz caster sugar
80g/3oz melted butter
100g/4oz plain white flour mixed with 4-5
teaspoons cold water to form a dough
Honey or golden syrup for glazing

Sieve the flour, spice and salt together and stir in
the yeast and sugar. Make a well in the centre of
the flour and add the milk, butter, lemon zest and
fruit and mix with a wooden spoon. Knead in all
the ingredients to form a smooth, elastic dough.
Continue to knead for 10 minutes. Divide the
dough into 12 equal parts, knead each one into
a roll and place on an oiled baking sheet. Flatten
slightly with the palm of your hand. Leave to
prove for 25-30 minutes.

Meanwhile, make a pastry type dough and roll
out into a rectangle measuring about 60cm/
24inches by 5cm/2inches. Cut into 24 strips
and, when the buns have finished proving,
brush them with a little water and put 2 strips of
pastry on each bun to form a cross, stretching
the strip to fit the bun. Bake for 10 minutes or
until cooked at 220°C/Gas mark 7. Brush each
bun with syrup or honey for a shiny finish. Serve
sliced with butter.

Chapter Nine
Cooking with Bread

Bread can be used as an ingredient or can play an important part in many recipes from croutons to puddings. It is so versatile it can be used to coat food and give it a crispy crust or as a binding ingredient in both sausages and burgers.

Bread can also be used in stuffings or sauces. What would a turkey dinner be without the bread sauce! Homemade pizza bases too taste so much better than bought ones and the quickest teatime dish is still 'something on toast.' It can be used as a thickening agent and even as a substitute utensil, ideal for mopping up the gravy from a stew.

Here are a few of my favourite ways of using bread in other recipes.

Home made Pizza Dough
(This is sufficient to make two large pizzas)

700g/1lb 8oz strong white flour or a mixture
of one third wholemeal and two thirds white
1 sachet fast acting dried yeast
2 teaspoons salt
Between 350ml/12fl oz and 450ml/15fl oz
warm water
1 tablespoon olive oil

Preheat the oven to its hottest setting. Sieve the flour and salt together into a bowl and stir in the dried yeast. Add half of the water and oil and stir well, mixing in more water to give a soft but workable dough. A greater quantity of water may be required if you are using wholemeal flour. Knead the dough for 10 minutes and leave to prove for 30 minutes. Divide the mixture into two and press and stretch each section to begin flattening the dough into pizza shapes. Use a rolling pin to finish off the shaping and place on an oiled baking sheet. Top with your favourite ingredients and bake at 200°C/Gas mark 6 for 20-25 minutes

To make the tomato pizza topping:

Combine 150ml/¼ pint passata with 1 crushed clove of garlic and 2 tablespoons of tomato puree. Stir well and add 1 tablespoon of olive oil. Herbs of your choice may also be added at this stage to vary the flavour. One teaspoon of dried or two heaped teaspoons of finely chopped fresh herbs will suffice.

The rest of the pizza toppings are up to you, but here are some of our favourites:

A mixture of mozzarella cheese and strong grated cheddar is our most popular cheese mixture.

A can of drained tuna, anchovies and black olives go together really well.

My personal favourite is tuna, lots of prawns and some thinly sliced red onion.

A vegetable special is finely chopped red and yellow peppers, thinly sliced courgettes, cut lengthways, and finely sliced spring onions with plenty of black pepper.

Chopped, smoked ham and sliced, fried mushrooms.

Pepperoni and chorizo sliced thinly with some scattered sun-dried tomatoes.

Joshua's Quick Pizza Toasties

1 tablespoon tomato puree
1 crushed clove garlic or ½ teaspoon garlic
puree
1 tablespoon olive oil
Any type of grated cheese to cover two slices of

bread
2 slices of good roast ham

Toast two slices of bread. Meanwhile, mix the tomato puree together with the garlic and oil. Spread the tomato mixture over the toast and arrange the slices of ham on top. If you prefer, chop the ham first. Sprinkle the cheese over the ham and toast under the grill for a few seconds until the cheese melts.

'Something on Toast'

This makes a really easy tea or lunch and is much more satisfying than a sandwich. Here are some ideas for toppings for your toast:

Sliced, fried mushrooms mixed with 2 tablespoons of crème fraiche and some chopped chives.

Cooked, chopped tomatoes in a little olive oil and sprinkled with a mixture of grated cheddar and cubed wenslydale cheese. The cheddar will melt but the wenslydale will remain in chunks.

Fry some chopped bacon and add some beaten eggs. Then simply scramble the eggs.

Mash some sardines with a little melted butter and black pepper and spread on your toast.

A quick Welsh rarebit type topping can be made by mixing 100g/4oz of cheddar cheese with two tablespoons of single cream, ½ a teaspoon of dry mustard powder and a beaten egg. Spread on top of lightly toasted bread and then grill until golden brown.

Mash some mackerel (a small tin) with a fork and add 2 tablespoons of cream cheese.

Eggy Bread

Eggy bread was always something we had with bacon when we didn't have enough eggs to go round. This is a tasty version of the old favourite and serves two people.

Beat two eggs with salt and pepper and two tablespoons of single cream. Dip two slices of bread in the mixture and fry on both sides in a little oil until golden brown and crispy. Serve with some good bacon and/or a couple of sausages.

Bread and Butter Puddings

There are many recipes for bread and butter pudding and everyone has their own favourite. I have never tasted one I didn't enjoy. Most are sweet pudding recipes but the first recipe I have chosen is for a cheesy bread and butter pudding.

The real secret to a great bread and butter pudding is to let it stand for 20-30 minutes before baking. This allows the bread to soak up all the liquid and the flavours, leaving a smoother, yet crustier finish to the pudding. Most recipes call for at least day old bread. I have tried it with newly bought, stale and everything in between and found the finished dish to be equally good, so don't worry too much about the age of the bread, so long as it hasn't started to go blue and furry!

The bread needs to be well buttered and each slice cut into four triangles. It is up to you whether you remove the crusts from the bread. For the Marmalade recipe it is best as it gives a smoother texture. They all serve about four people.

Savoury Bread and Butter Pudding

4 slices wholemeal bread, well buttered
3 eggs, well beaten
175g/6oz strong flavoured cheese, grated
1 teaspoon dry mustard powder
225ml/8fl oz milk
2 tablespoons freshly chopped chives
$1/2$ teaspoon salt
Lots of ground black pepper

Butter an ovenproof dish and place the bread and butter slices in the dish, overlapping them evenly. Scatter the chives over the bread. Mix the eggs, milk and mustard powder together and add the salt. Pour over the bread and season with black pepper. Leave to stand for 20 minutes. Sprinkle the cheese over the top and bake at 190°C/Gas mark 5 for 30-40 minutes or until the mixture is set. Serve with a green salad or some roasted tomatoes.

Basic Bread and Butter Pudding

4 slices white bread, de-crusted and well
buttered
80g/3oz currants
3 eggs, beaten
280ml/½ pint milk
Zest of 1 lemon
2 teaspoons vanilla extract
50g/2oz unrefined granulated sugar
Grated nutmeg

Cut each slice into four triangles and arrange the bread in layers, butter side up in a buttered ovenproof dish. Sprinkle the currants over each layer of bread. Beat the milk, vanilla and lemon zest into the eggs, add the sugar and stir well. Pour over the bread. Add a little grated nutmeg to the top and leave to stand for 30 minutes, Then bake for 30-40 minutes at 190°C/Gas mark 5 until well risen with a crusty top. If you like a very crusty top to your pudding, sprinkle with a little extra caster sugar before the nutmeg.

Marmalade Bread and Butter Pudding

This is a luxurious variation of the pudding and well worth making for a special occasion. The recipe calls for Cointreau, but brandy or rum would do equally well.

4 slices white or brown bread, de- crusted and
buttered
Seville orange marmalade for spreading
3 eggs
2 tablespoons single cream
350ml/12fl oz milk
50g/2oz raisins
1 tablespoon Cointreau
1 tablespoon brown sugar
Zest of 1 orange
A little extra sugar for sprinkling

Spread the marmalade onto the bread slices.
Arrange the bread in layers in a well buttered
oven proof dish and scatter raisins over each layer
of bread. Sprinkle the sugar over the bread.
Beat the eggs and add the milk, cream, orange
zest and Cointreau. Pour the mixture over the
bread and leave to stand for 20 minutes.
Bake for 30-40 minutes at 190°C/Gas mark 5
until set and golden brown. Serve with double
cream laced with a little Cointreau.

Chocolate Bread and Butter Pudding

This is another deliciously different take on the
old favourite. It uses brioche instead of bread, but
still butter the slices as it gives a moister finish.
Brioche comes in all sizes so use the equivalent
amount of brioche as you would bread. You may
add a tablespoon of brandy to give it an extra
dimension.

4 slices of brioche
3 eggs, beaten
300ml/½ pint milk
150ml/¼ pint single cream
1 x 100g/4oz bar high cocoa content dark
chocolate broken into small pieces
1 tablespoon brown caster sugar
Extra chocolate for topping the pudding

Place your buttered brioche into a buttered ovenproof dish and sprinkle with the sugar.
Warm the milk and cream in a pan and add the chocolate when the liquid has reached body heat. Continue to heat gently until the chocolate has melted and remove from the heat. Vigorously beat in the eggs and pour over the brioche. Leave to stand for 10 minutes.
Bake for 30-40 minutes at 190°C/Gas mark 5 until set. Just before the cooking time is finished grate some extra chocolate over the pudding and finish cooking. Serve cold or warm with cream.

Bread Pudding

This is similar to a bread and butter pudding, but the bread is broken into small pieces rather than left in slices. It combines the flavours of apple, cinnamon and dried fruit and is a very comforting dessert when served with custard. It is cut into squares and serves about 6 – 8 people.

8 slices white bread
4 eggs, beaten
280ml/½ pint milk
1 dessert apple, grated with a squeeze of lemon
juice
350g/12oz mixed dried fruit
3 tablespoons soft, brown sugar
2 tablespoons Seville orange marmalade
1 level teaspoon ground cinnamon
1 level teaspoon mixed spice
120g/4oz butter

Break the bread into small pieces and put it in a mixing bowl. Pour over the milk and leave for 20 minutes. Mash well with a fork to smooth out the lumps of bread. Add the grated apple to the bread mixture and stir in the dried fruit, sugar, marmalade, spices and eggs.
Melt the butter and add half to the bread mixture and beat well. Pour the pudding mixture into a buttered ovenproof dish and drizzle the rest of the melted butter over the top.
Bake for 1-1½ hours at 180°C/Gas mark 4. Check the pudding regularly after 1 hour. It needs to be firm and golden brown.

Apple and Blackberry Charlotte

Apple charlotte was an old school favourite of mine and then one day I was in a restaurant and ordered apple and blackberry charlotte - it was amazing. I have developed this version over the years in memory of that gorgeous dessert.

The Bread and Butter Book

8 thin slices white bread, de-crusted
2 medium sized Bramley apples
220g/8oz blackberries
50g/2oz butter
2 tablespoons lemon juice
180g/6oz sugar
Butter for frying
1 tablespoon caster sugar for sprinkling over the pudding

Peel, core and slice the apples and place them in a pan with the blackberries, sugar, butter and lemon juice. Simmer for approximately 10 minutes until the apples begin to 'fall.'
Cut each slice of bread into three equal strips and fry gently in the butter until crisp and golden.
Butter a deep soufflé type dish and line it with the fried bread. Cover the bottom and the sides. Pour in the fruit mixture and cover with the remaining bread strips. Sprinkle the top with caster sugar and bake for 20-25 minutes at 190°C/Gas mark 5. Serve with custard or cream.

Summer Fruit Pudding

This is a real 'ooh' and 'aah' type of pudding and one of the easiest to make, yet it is an awesome looking dessert. It does need to be made the day before you wish to serve it, so it does need a bit of planning.

750g/1½ lbs prepared mixed summer fruits; strawberries, raspberries, redcurrants,

blackcurrants or de-stoned cherries
50g/2oz unrefined caster sugar
8 slices white bread, de-crusted

Stew the fruit in 60ml/2fl oz of water with the sugar. Cut the bread to line a buttered pudding basin, cutting out a circle for the bottom. Make sure you overlap each piece of bread to form a seal to hold in the fruit. Pour the hot fruit into the basin, being careful not to disturb the bread. Keep some of the juice to pour over the pudding just before serving. The pudding needs to be full of fruit before topping it with a bread lid.
Allow to cool and cover it with a plate, leaving it to chill overnight in the fridge. Serve with cream.

Autumn Fruit Pudding

This is prepared in the same way as the summer fruit pudding. Use the same ingredients but substitute the summer fruits for a mixture of the following; plums, pears, apples and blackberries.

Brown Betty Puddings

These are similar to crumbles but use breadcrumbs instead of a crumble topping. They are easy to prepare and go well with lots of different fruits.

Rhubarb Brown Betty

450g/1lb rhubarb, trimmed and cut into pieces

230g/8oz freshly made wholemeal
breadcrumbs
50g/2oz brown sugar
25g/1oz unrefined caster sugar
1 level teaspoon ground ginger
2 tablespoons orange juice, either fresh or from
a carton

Stew the rhubarb with the caster sugar for a few minutes until the rhubarb is just soft. Meanwhile, combine the breadcrumbs, brown sugar and ginger in a bowl. When the rhubarb is cooked, place it in a buttered ovenproof dish. Pour over the breadcrumb mixture evenly and drizzle the orange juice over the crumbs. Bake for 30-40 minutes at 170°C/Gas mark 3 until the top is golden brown.

Gooseberry Brown Betty

450g/1lb gooseberries, topped and tailed
80g/3oz Muscovado sugar
1 dessertspoon elderflower cordial mixed with 2
tablespoons water
230g/8oz freshly made brown breadcrumbs
50g/2oz brown sugar

Stew the gooseberries with the sugar until tender. Mix the breadcrumbs with the brown sugar. Pour the fruit into a buttered dish and sprinkle over the crumb mixture, drizzling the crumbs with the elderflower juice. Bake for 30-40 minutes at 170°C/Gasmark 3 until golden brown.

Serve Brown Betty puddings with cream or custard, either hot or cold. They even taste good the next day if covered and stored in a cool place.

Croutons

Croutons are great served with soups, salads or pasta dishes and making your own is very simple. You don't need to deep-fry them and they can be made in the oven. If you do deep fry them, which is quicker, only fry them for a few seconds in very hot fat to keep them crisp but not oily. They can also be shallow fried but sometimes you just don't want another pan on the stove.

To make crispy, yet dry croutons for two people:

2 slices of white or brown bread, cut into cubes
4 tablespoons olive oil
Salt to taste

Place the olive oil in a bowl and add the bread. Coat well in the oil and spread on a baking sheet. Season with salt and place in a hot oven at 220°C/Gas mark 7 until they are golden. Drain on kitchen paper if necessary and serve.

Parmesan Croutons

These are delicious served with tomato based pasta dishes. They are made in the same way as above but sprinkle with finely grated Parmesan cheese and a little black pepper.

Herb croutons

Serve these with soups and salads of all kinds. Prepare in the same way as the first recipe but sprinkle a mixture of your favourite herbs over the croutons together with a little salt.

Garlic croutons

These can be served with just about anything if you like garlic. Finely chop 2 cloves of garlic, mix it with 1 teaspoon of salt and sprinkle it over the croutons. Again, cook as above.

Breadcrumb Coatings

Breadcrumbs can be used for many different kinds of food coatings for frying fish or chicken or when roasting meats. Try the following the next time you do a roast:

For Lamb
Herb and Mustard Coating

200g/7oz breadcrumbs
1 tablespoon chopped parsley
1 teaspoon dried rosemary
2 tablespoons wholegrain mustard
Salt and pepper to taste

Mix all the ingredients together and press over the joint before cooking. Season to taste.

For Beef
Horseradish Coating

200g/7oz breadcrumbs
1 teaspoon Dijon mustard
1 teaspoon white wine vinegar
2 tablespoons grated horseradish
4 tablespoons double cream

Mix all the ingredients together and press over a beef joint or over steaks as they are frying. Cook the side to be coated first, then turn over and coat each steak. The quantities given will coat four average sized steaks.

For Pork
Apricot and Sage Coating

200g/7oz breadcrumbs
150g/5oz dried apricots, chopped very finely
3 tablespoons soy sauce
1 dessertspoon chopped fresh sage
1 tablespoon balsamic vinegar

Score the skin or fat on the joint. Mix all the other ingredients together and press well into the meat before roasting. This goes particularly well with a belly pork joint that is cooked for a long time.

Good old Sage and Onion Stuffing

Yes we can buy the packet mix and quite honestly I love the most famous one of all and do use it for speed sometimes. But there is nothing to beat a homemade sage and onion stuffing to serve with either poultry or pork.

2 small onions or 1 large, finely chopped
100g/4oz fresh white breadcrumbs
2 tablespoons freshly chopped sage leaves
Salt and pepper to taste
Butter for frying

Fry the onion in a little butter until soft and allow to cool. Add the breadcrumbs, sage leaves, salt and pepper. Use to accompany your favourite roasted poultry or pork joint.
Other stuffings to try are Mushroom and Thyme, Lemon and Parsley and Mixed Herb.

Mushroom and Thyme

1 medium onion, chopped finely
100g/4oz open-cup mushrooms, chopped well
100g/4oz fresh white breadcrumbs
1 tablespoon fresh or 1 teaspoon dried thyme
Salt and pepper
Butter for frying

Fry the onion until soft and add the mushrooms. Continue cooking until most of the mushroom moisture has cooked away. Then simply add the breadcrumbs, thyme, salt and pepper.

Lemon and Parsley

Juice and zest of 1 lemon
Two tablespoons chopped fresh parsley
100g/4oz white breadcrumbs
2 tablespoon melted butter
Salt and pepper to taste

Combine all the ingredients and mix well. Season to taste. This stuffing goes particularly well with belly pork. Before rolling a joint of belly pork, spread the meat with the stuffing.

Finally, what Christmas dinner would be complete without the traditional Bread Sauce.

Traditional Bread Sauce

2 shallots, chopped
50g/2oz butter
50g/2oz white breadcrumbs
300ml/½ pint milk
1 tablespoon single cream
1 bay leaf
4 cloves
Salt and black pepper

Put the milk, cream, shallots, bay leaf, cloves, salt and black pepper into a pan and bring to the boil. As soon as it boils, remove from the heat and allow the flavours to infuse the milk. This should take about half an hour. Reheat the mixture and pour over the breadcrumbs, straining all the debris away as you do so.

Add the butter to the mixture and stir well. Serve immediately.

Chapter Ten
When Things Go Wrong

As with anything you do, there are things that can go wrong in bread making, especially if you are just starting out. I still make mistakes and sometimes have the odd disaster. Just recently I forgot to put the yeast in my mixture and wondered why it was taking so long to get to the correct texture during kneading. It was only when I found my yeast sachet behind my very large mixing bowl that I realised what I had done. I was able to incorporate it into my dough but it took some time and the finished product wasn't as good as usual and didn't have the usual soft inside, but we still ate it.

The Bread and Butter Book

There are many things that can go wrong in bread making; some are minor problems which can be rectified easily but others are disastrous. This chapter will try and explain some of these problems and how they can be dealt with successfully. I always feel that wasting food is a crying shame and shouldn't happen, so read on to prevent you possibly having to throw away a batch of bread. I have also included some ideas for creatively using up any disasters.

The Mixing

The only real problem you may encounter at this stage is with the yeast. If you are using fresh yeast or ordinary dried yeast and it hasn't started frothing up after ten or fifteen minutes then the yeast is probably dead. This could be because it wasn't fresh to begin with or because the water was too hot when making the ferment and has perhaps killed the yeast. So a fresh batch will need to be prepared with cooler water or another piece of fresher yeast or a new sachet of dried yeast.

The temperature of the liquid used in recipes calling for fast action yeast is also very important as the heat of the liquid will kill the yeast in the dough if it is too hot. The best way to tell is to dip your finger in the liquid. It should feel warm. If it feels hot this will kill the yeast before it has had a chance to work. The other ingredient that can affect the yeast is salt. This slows down the fermenting ability of the yeast and, if in too close contact with the yeast, will also kill it. So it is important to mix the salt into the flour thoroughly before adding the yeast or yeast mixture. This will ensure that the salt and yeast come into

136

minimum contact during the making of the bread.

The warmth of the room and your cooking utensils may also affect the speed and efficiency of the yeast. Though yeast will carry on working when the atmosphere is chilled it is slowed down greatly. This can be an advantage if you want to prove your bread slowly (more about that in a later chapter), but for faster results it is best to work in a warm atmosphere.

Another problem can be too little or too much liquid. The former is very easy to rectify by gradually adding a little more liquid. It is important to carry on mixing as you add the liquid because this is the time when it can easily become too much. If you do add too much, keep mixing and begin to knead the dough. If it is still too sticky, add a little more flour, but just a small handful at a time. DO NOT POUR STRAIGHT FROM THE BAG! The dough is better sticky than dry as it will be soft and light when cooked, whereas a dry dough will end up as heavy and indigestible.

Always take care when adding salt. Do not guess the quantity. The recipe will be very clear as to how much salt should be added. Too much will spoil the bread as I have learnt to my cost in the past.

The Kneading

Kneading must be done properly for 10 minutes to allow the gluten in the flour to develop and produce the soft, springy texture of bread. The soft and sticky mixture will become a spongy dough as you knead it.

If this doesn't happen continue kneading a bit more vigorously. It should become smooth and springy and the stickiness should go. Add a little more flour if it is still too sticky after 5 or 6 minutes of kneading. You will know after baking bread a few times just when the consistency of the kneaded dough is correct.

The Proving

There are two main problems that can occur when bread is left to rise. The first is not leaving it for long enough and of course the other is leaving it too long.

Leaving it too long is easy to see as the dough loses its shape and sags over to one side or spreads and flattens down. You will be left with odd shapes that don't cook evenly. There is very little you can do to rectify this so keep an eye on the time and check the dough regularly during proving.

Not leaving it long enough isn't as much of a problem for the finished product. The bread will be slightly heavier than it should be, but the overall effect will still be edible.

The secret to timing the proving accurately is to keep checking it and, when the dough has doubled in size, it is ready to either bake or knock back depending on the recipe you are using.

Knocking Back

This is only necessary in recipes which use fresh or ordinary dried yeast. By this time the dough shouldn't be sticky so don't flour your board too much for the knocking back as this can cause streaks of flour in the finished bread. A light dusting of flour is all that is required at this stage.

To ensure an even distribution of gas throughout the loaf, knock out the large pockets of gas with your fist quickly till it is smooth and give another gentle knead till the dough has regained its elasticity. The bread will now be ready to finish rising evenly without any large pockets of gas to spoil its shape.

The Shaping

Remember that as the dough rises it will lose some of itse original shape so don't waste time putting on fancy patterns or making complicated shapes. Start with a simple one that keeps its shape whilst proving. Don't be tempted to alter your bread's shape during the proving process as this can spoil the finished bread as it interferes with the gas flow through the bread and the shape will never recover.

The Second Proving

There is very little that can go wrong with this that I have not already mentioned. Just keep checking the dough and when it has doubled in size it is ready for baking.

The Baking

Knowing your oven is the key to success here. Bread needs to be cooked at a high temperature to kill the yeast but you don't want to burn the dough. You will know where the hottest part of your oven is and this is where the bread needs to be placed at the temperature given in the recipe. Keep checking the bread after 10 minutes. Don't worry – opening the door won't make it won't fall like sponge cake so it isn't detrimental to the finished loaf. If the loaf is browning too quickly on the top, lower its position in the oven. After 10 minutes has passed the temperature may also be lowered slightly so that the bread finishes cooking but doesn't burn.

Under cooking bread is unsatisfactory as the yeast will still be able to work and the bread will be inedible. So if the bread isn't brown on the crust, leave it in the oven for a longer time. Larger loaves often look cooked but when you slice them they are under cooked in the centre. This can be remedied by lowering the temperature by a few degrees after the initial cooking time of 10-15 minutes, allowing the bread to cook evenly and ensuring the yeast has been properly killed.

If your loaf is burnt on the bottom it is either that the baking tin or tray is too thin or the bread is too low in the oven. So bake your loaf using two or three sheets of baking parchment or greaseproof paper under the loaf whilst baking. If baking in a tin place it on a baking sheet as extra protection from the heat. If it is too low then bake the loaf in the centre of the oven to ensure an even spread of heat.

Incidentally, this is the origin of the phrase 'upper crust.' In the large stone ovens the 'peasants' got the bottom loaves which were usually burnt, whilst the gentry got the loaves from the top.

After Baking

Once your bread is cooked there is only one thing that can go wrong. It is very tempting to slice your bread as soon as you can after it is removed from the oven, However, this is not a good idea. If it is a large loaf the bread will squash down with the pressure of the knife and your hand and will never regain its shape again. If it is a small cob or roll then when you cut into it the middle section of dough will come away from the crust in a ball and lose its shape. So wait for at least 15 minutes for small rolls and 25 minutes or longer for larger loaves.

Using up your Disasters

Have you have added too much or too little salt?
Make crumbs and use them to thicken soups, curries and stews. You will not need to add as much salt to the dish if any at all, just do the taste test.
Use the crumbs to coat fish or chicken. When frying again don't salt the food beforehand.
These two ideas can also be used if you have forgotten to add salt as the process is simply reversed.

Has your loaf been proving too long and toppled over?
Very gently ease the dough into a bakeable shape and cook as normal. It will have lost some of its lightness but will still taste good. This is better eaten

fairly soon after baking, whilst still soft. After cooling for about 30 minutes eat with soup or salads. If it is difficult to slice then serve it as a 'tear and share' loaf. Alternatively, cut it into thick slices as best you can and spread some chopped garlic over it along with a drizzle of extra virgin olive oil and you have a delicious garlic bread that no one will care what shape it is as it will taste so good.

Has the bread burnt on the bottom or the top of the loaf?

The best way to deal with this is after slicing. Don't be tempted to cut the burnt bit off whole. It is much easier to get rid of the burnt bit after cutting a slice and just trimming any unwanted crust. If it is dark brown you probably won't need to cut too much off. If it is black you will need to remove all the blackened bit as eating carbon isn't very good for you!

Has the bread remained raw in the middle?

Sometimes a loaf can look raw and still smell yeasty in the middle, even when the rest of the loaf seems cooked. It is best not to eat this section. It may be cut away after slicing or, if it is a large loaf, slice the whole thing in two and make a 'tartine' type sandwich. Simply cut away the raw bit and fill it with delicious things, replace the top and tie some string around it to secure it, then cover it with foil. Place some weights from your scales securely on top to press the loaf and leave it for an hour or so before slicing. This is delicious with a picnic.

Symptom	Solution
Yeasty taste	Either too much yeast or not cooked at a high enough temperature
knobbly top during proving	Knead for longer and more evenly
Taking a long time to rise	Needs a warmer place to prove
Not crusty	Brush the dough during cooking time with a salt water solution: ½ teaspoon salt to 4 tablespoons warm water.
Very heavy texture	Add a little more liquid next time and ensure the dough is kneaded for at least 10 minutes
Loaf has fallen to one side during proving	Rising too quickly, in too warm a place or too much yeast has been added. Support the dough and bake
Doesn't have much flavour	Not enough salt added to the mixture
Big air bubbles in the centre of the loaf.	Not kneaded vigorously enough.

Chapter Eleven
Growing Wheat

You would not be surprised to read that the loaf of bread you make from flour comes largely from the air, converted into starch and protein by wheat and converted into food by ourselves. But quite how this process takes place is part mystery, part science and part hard work. What might be a surprise is the fact that this process can take place in your own garden. It is possible for you to go from the seed right through to the loaf, and almost everyone in the world has the skill.

Wheat, like all cereals, is simply a special grass. The lawns we almost all have could easily be wheat.

The yield of wheat from two square metres of land would be just enough to give you a large loaf. You would need a large allotment to grow enough to produce enough bread to feed a family of four, and then you would also need some way of storing it and another couple of allotments to maintain a crop rotation. The whole idea of growing your own wheat is not really relevant when we can buy it so cheaply from around the world, but even the least outrageous forecasts show that, as we approach the end of the first decade of the 21st century, bread wheat will become in shorter and shorter supply. The time when we need to grow our own wheat may well be upon us sooner than we might think.

In Victorian times, when the last of the common land had all been siphoned off to make large farms, the poor had no land to grow their meagre crops. The Church came to the rescue by providing allotments for families to enable them to provide for themselves. Largely these allotments were planted with wheat for bread. Potatoes and vegetables were usually grown at home. Growing wheat is in our blood.

Varieties

Wheat has been produced from simple ancestors; Emmer in the south of Europe and in Asia Minor, North Africa and Egypt and Einkorn in the mountainous north of Europe. As people moved out to new habitats their wheat went with them. The problems faced by differing climates and terrains were solved by crossing wheat varieties so that specific plants thrived for the people who grew them. In India it is said that there are some 2000 varieties of wheat and other cereals such as rice.Modern wheat has taken the art of former years and made a science out of them. New varieties have been produced with financial considerations in mind rather than solely habitat or agriculture. For example, as combine harvesters replaced scythes as the means of harvesting, so the stem size of modern wheat was shortened to make the crop easier to collect. Similarly, easy drying wheat has replaced some of the earlier rougher types, saving money on the blowing/drying process in wet summers. But the home grower of wheat need not worry about such matters as, in the main, they will probably not be doing it for hugely commercial reasons.

Wheat comes in two varieties; spring and winter. Winter wheat is sown in autumn and is in the ground for around ten months and is harvested the following summer. Spring wheat is sown in the spring and is harvested in the late summer. The winter wheat produces a better crop so it is best to use this if you can. When sown it starts to grow under the last heat of the summer and then, when only a few inches high, it stops growing. The spring then heralds further vigorous growth and you get much stronger plants.

You can buy 25kg bags of winter wheat from seed suppliers. For bread making you must ask for a hard wheat such as 'Mascot' or 'Solstice' but the truth is that you can also make good bread from soft wheat too.

Preparing the ground

You need bare earth. Dig over the ground and then chop it. You are looking for a fine, crumbly texture. When you have done this youwill need to rake the soil so that it is smooth and fine. Land from a previous crop (potatoes are a good one) is ideal. You can simply dig this over and rake it to make a tilth. You can sow spring wheat in April or winter wheat in September. You broadcast the seed so that the soil is evenly covered and looks as though you have peppered it. Then you rake it in, or use a brush as you would if you were making a fine lawn.

You need to have used up about half a 25kg bag per large allotment; a good handful and a half per square metre. On a field scale you are probably better using a seeder. They seem a bit extravagant but there is nothing better. They give a very even spread and at the same time provide a very measured amount of seed. They are not that expensive and if you are doing this every year it is clearly money well spent.

Harvest

The crop will yellow as it ripens and by late August it is ready for harvest. The grains in the heads ripen and swell. At first they are what is called 'milky ripe' around six to eight weeks before harvest is ready. If you thrust your thumb nail into the seeds they will ooze a milky liquid. The grain is ready when it is hard, dry and will rub out of the head in the hands. Traditionally the crop is cut at ground level with a scythe. You can also use a sharp knife or a sickle if you like. It is hard work but you need to keep at it if you want to get all the grain in before it rains. You cannot afford for it to go black with fungus, which is what happens when the grain is wet.

The grain is beaten out of the heads. This is called threshing. Some people use a flail which is simply two stout sticks hinged in the middle with a chain or some leather. Put a large cloth on the soil (not concrete because you'll bash a hole in it) and spread the wheat on this by the armful. Then bash it until all the seed is out. You can also use the back of a chair to bash the grain out. Simply put the chair on the cloth – an old sheet will do – and take all your frustrations out on the chair with the wheat.

Finally, give the grain a good rub to release any sticky chaff and then, over the sheet on a windy day, throw the grain into the air. The wind will blow the chaff away.

Wheat needs to be stored dry in sacks where any excess moisture can escape. If you do not have any special storage tanks, check the wheat from time to time for dryness.

Grinding

This can be done in a pestle and mortar if you have the patience but using a coffee grinder is much easier. Easier still is a purpose built grinder which you can buy either hand cranked or electrically driven. But do not make too much flour at a time. Wheat keeps much better as a seed than as flour.

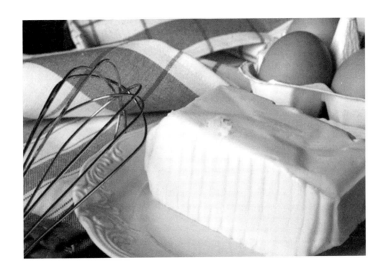

Chapter Twelve
Making Butter

In our present health obsessed society why would anyone want to make their own butter?

As with any other foodstuff, moderation is the key. Unless you have a medical reason for not consuming animal fats then butter is actually better for you than hydrogenated fats and the flavour is certainly much more appealing than most margarines. It is also a very versatile ingredient and, when combined with olive oil in frying, the taste is unmatched. To be able to make your own butter in whatever quantity you require and to be certain of its freshness is reason enough to have a go.

Finally, it makes you feel very clever! When I go

out to schools and show children the simple art of butter making they (and usually the teachers too!) are enthralled by the simple 'magic' of turning liquid into solid.

To be able to put on the table your own bread <u>and</u> your own butter is a wonderful experience.

I was amazed at the 'magic' trick my husband performed for me one day. 'Watch this!' he said. After a few minutes of shaking what I thought was a bottle of milk up and down he stopped, cut the plastic open and poured some liquid into a bowl, then scooped out the rest of its contents. 'There, taste that. It's butter,' he exclaimed and he was right. It tasted just like the butter I had bought the previous day to make a cake, the unsalted type.

To Make Basic Butter

500ml carton of double cream
An empty 2 litre plastic milk bottle

Pour the carton of cream into the bottle and put the lid back on very bottle securely. Now shake it up and down as fast and as vigorously as you can. It is good exercise!

Keep the shaking going till you hear the cream separate. This sounds like a heavy thud in the bottle together with the splashing sound of the newly separated liquid. Don't get disheartened if it's turned to whipped cream and doesn't seem to be getting anywhere – simply keep on shaking and shaking and it will turn quite suddenly.

Then take off the lid and pour the liquid into a jug . Cut round the widest part of the bottle and scoop out the solid mass that is left. It will look like butter and smell like it too because it is butter!.

You will need to 'wash off' the rest of the buttermilk (that is the liquid that is left after it has separated) by using a fine holed metal colander. You can use a plastic one but I find metal ones are easier to de-grease afterwards. Put the butter in the colander and cut into it gently whilst holding it under a tap of gently running cold water. Keep the water at a steady stream; not too fast or else it forces the butter through the holes.

Shake off the excess water and place on a clean, cold surface; a marble chopping board is ideal but a plate will do. Mix in a teaspoon of salt and chop into the butter, mixing in the salt as you go. Pile the mixture together in the centre and squeeze and push it down, allowing more liquid out. The more buttermilk you can get out, the longer the product will keep and the taste will be better. If you need unsalted butter for a recipe then this is the stage when you can put it into a clean dish or a large ramekin. If you prefer to salt the butter, add another level teaspoon and mix well. Taste and add more salt if necessary. Once salted, place it in a container, cover it with greaseproof paper and store in the fridge. Use it within a week to spread on bread or to cook with, either frying or baking.

If you add more salt the butter will keep better, but after tasting your home made butter it will soon be consumed.

You may find that adding a teaspoon of crème fraiche to the bottle with the cream before shaking will balance the finished flavour of the butter. I have found this enhances the flavour of ordinary cream, but if you use jersey cream it probably won't need it. This addition of crème fraiche gives a little acidity to the butter which helps the flavour of the end product.

The best thing to do is to experiment and find the taste you prefer, I like using Jersey cream best as my family enjoys the flavour of the butter spread on bread. For baking, however, I prefer to use non-Jersey cream.

You can use double the amount of cream at the beginning if you wish to make more butter, but the milk bottle is not large enough to make a larger quantity. If you want to make more you will need to purchase a butter churn. This is a container made either of glass, plastic, pottery or metal, although historically they were made of wood. The most modern ones are usually plastic or metal but we have a glass one that is about fifty years old and very efficient. The container holds around half a gallon of cream and has a lid to which is attached a paddle which goes inside the container. By turning the handle you can churn the cream to make the butter. This still requires a bit of elbow grease and I find it takes longer than using the plastic bottle method, but if you want to make a larger quantity of product they are very useful. I find I can make a week's worth of butter freshly without much hassle by using the bottle method, plus it has the added bonus of re-using something that would be discarded by recycling of course. Butter will also freeze.

If you want to make a pat of butter, a pair of 'scotch hands' is useful. These are wooden paddles with ridges running along the length of them. They are used to remove the last dregs of buttermilk and to shape the butter. You will need to practise using these as they can be quite tricky. I find that, so long as the butter is well rinsed, I don't bother with my scotch hands as I put the butter straight into my dish.

When you have made your butter you can add various ingredients to it to enhance other foodstuffs. I like to do this soon after I have made it but it makes no difference so long as you take it out of the fridge beforehand to soften it. The best way to soften butter for the following recipes is to cream it in a bowl with a plastic, silicone or wooden spatula or a baking spoon.

Parsley Butter

125g butter
1 heaped tablespoon of chopped fresh parsley
Salt to taste

Freshly ground pepper to taste
Juice of half a lemon

Mash the butter gently in a bowl, working it till soft. Blend in the parsley and add the salt, pepper and lemon juice. This can be used to flavour fish and meats, but I think it goes particularly well with vegetables. After cooking carrots, swede and beetroots, add a generous knob of parsley butter and serve. Delicious!

Many other ingredients may be added in place of parsley. Other herbs such as mint, basil, chervil, tarragon, thyme or dill all make a simple sauce for many foods. If you use rosemary or sage take care with the amount you use as they have a much more concentrated flavour and can be too overpowering if you are too heavy handed. As an alternative to herbs the following ingredients also make excellent butter garnishes:

3-4 crushed garlic cloves
6 anchovy fillets, mashed well
1teaspoon of paprika
1 level teaspoon of cumin and the same of
coriander make a good addition to curries
2 teaspoons of mustard
2 teaspoons of coarsely ground black
pepper goes well with a fried beefsteak

Watercress Butter

Pour boiling water over 100g watercress, then

plunge in cold water. Purée, add to 150g of softened butter and season with salt and black pepper to taste. This is delicious spread on bread for egg sandwiches.

Roquefort Butter

Mix 100g Roquefort cheese with a tablespoon of brandy, using a fork to work the cheese into the liquid. Add a level teaspoon of mustard and work into 150g softened butter. Use to garnish savoury pastries or canapés.

Rum Butter

At Christmas rum and brandy butters are traditionally served with puddings and mince pies.

200g butter
100g soft brown sugar
Nutmeg
4 tablespoons rum

Cream the butter until soft and beat in the sugar and nutmeg. Add the rum slowly so that the mixture doesn't curdle and beat thoroughly.

Brandy Butter

100g butter
30g soft brown sugar
4 tablespoons brandy

The Bread and Butter Book

Cream the butter and sugar together till fluffy and add the brandy gradually.

Butter is also used to make a roux to thicken sauces. Blend an equal quantity of butter and sifted plain flour and add gradually, in small amounts, to warmed liquids. Alternatively, melt the butter in a pan over a low heat, then remove the pan from the heat and add the flour. Return to the heat and add the warmed liquid as required. Quantities for a roux mix are 15g of butter and 15g of plain flour to ½ pint of liquid.

Buerre Blanc

Another classic butter sauce recipe is a buerre blanc, or white butter, which is delicious served with fish.

100ml white wine vinegar
100ml dry white wine
2 large shallots, chopped
Salt and pepper to taste
200ml melted butter

Add the vinegar, wine and shallots to a pan and reduce. Allow to cool slightly and whisk in the butter gradually. Strain into a sauceboat or other serving vessel.

Clarified Butter

This is used for frying foods and in emulsified

sauces. This is made by heating the butter gently in a heavy based saucepan. Do not stir but allow it to heat until the butter stops spitting. This indicates that all the water has evaporated. There will be a little white coloured sediment left in the bottom of the pan. If you pour the butter carefully into a container, leave this residue behind and discard it. Clarified butter, or ghee, is often used in Asian dishes for frying meats and vegetables.

Noisette Butter

This is also known as meunière butter and is made by heating the desired amount in a frying pan until it is golden brown and produces a nutty smell. It can then be served piping hot with strong flavoured fish, vegetables that have been pre-cooked or eggs.

Before making soups I always sweat my vegetables in a large knob of butter as I think it creates a better flavour than simply adding liquid to the prepared ingredients. If you cook your vegetables in butter and a little salt and pepper over a very low heat for about 20 minutes, this will draw out the lovely juices of the vegetables. Then add the liquid stock and finish cooking the soup in the regular way.

Orange Butter

1/2 cup softened butter
1 tbsp orange juice

1 teaspoon grated orange peel

Combine the butter, orange juice, and orange peel and blend well.

Almond Butter

1/2 cup softened butter
1 tablespoon finely chopped almonds
1/2 teaspoon almond extract

Mix all the ingredients together. Use this almond butter with quick breads and muffins, pancakes, and other breads.

Horseradish Butter

$1/4$ cup butter, softened
$1^1/_2$ teaspoons prepared mustard
1 teaspoon prepared horseradish
A dash of ground black pepper

Combine all the ingredients and cream until light and fluffy. Mix in with mashed potato.

Sage Butter

12 fresh sage leaves
100g/$3^1/_2$oz butter, softened
4 teaspoons wholegrain mustard
salt and freshly ground black pepper

Cream all the ingredients together and chill in the fridge. Use as a filling for pork or chicken fillets/Kievs.

Potted Shrimps

When I was a child one of my favourite treats was to go to Southport for the day and my Dad would buy some potted shrimps. We would go home and have them with hot toasted bread for tea. I decided recently to make my own. It is very quick, easy and absolutely delicious.

Simply place 200g shrimps in a small dish and pour over 50g of melted, home-made butter mixed with ½ teaspoon of cayenne pepper or paprika pepper if you prefer a smokey rather than a spicy taste.

Butter is a very versatile ingredient and being able to make your own is the perfect accompaniment to your home-made bread. To make sufficient cream for your butter will, however, require at least a gallon of milk, so owning a family cow would be ideal. Other than that spotting any reduced price double cream is an inexpensive and perhaps easier option.

Traditionally cream is made by allowing the milk to stand and the top of the milk [the cream] is then skimmed off. The cream is pasteurised and left to mature. This can then be used to make butter either by using a churn or by the method explained in this chapter.

The Good Life Press
P O Box 536
Preston
PR2 9ZY
01772 652693

The Good Life Press publishes a wide range of titles for the smallholder, farmer and country dweller as well as Home Farmer, the monthly magazine aimed at anyone who wants to grab a slice of the good life - whether they live in the country or the city.

Other Titles of interest

A Guide to Traditional Pig Keeping by Carol Harris
An Introduction to Keeping Cattle by Peter King
An Introduction to Keeping Sheep by J Upton/D Soden
Build It! by Joe Jacobs
Cider Making by Andrew Lea
First Find a Field by Rosamund Young
Flowerpot Farming by Jayne Neville
Grow and Cook by Brian Tucker
How to Butcher Livestock and Game by Paul Peacock
Making Jams and Preserves by Diana Sutton
Precycle! by Paul Peacock
Showing Sheep by Sue Kendrick
Talking Sheepdogs by Derek Scrimgeour
The Bread and Butter Book by Diana Sutton
The Cheese Making Book By Paul Peacock
The Pocket Book of Wild Food by Paul Peacock
The Polytunnel Companion by Jayne Neville
The Sausage Book by Paul Peacock
The Shepherd's Companion by Jane Upton
The Smoking and Curing Book by Paul Peacock
The Urban Farmer's Handbook by Paul Peacock

www.goodlifepress.co.uk
www.homefarmer.co.uk